# School House
*to*
## *White House*

### THE EDUCATION OF THE PRESIDENTS

D1472854

# School House

## to

## White House

### THE EDUCATION OF THE PRESIDENTS

FROM THE HOLDINGS
OF THE NATIONAL ARCHIVES
PRESIDENTIAL LIBRARIES

The Foundation for the National Archives, Washington DC
in association with D Giles Limited, London

Copyright © 2007 The Foundation for the National Archives
First published in 2007 by GILES
an imprint of D Giles Limited
2nd Floor,
162-164 Upper Richmond Road,
London, SW15 2SL, UK
www.gilesltd.com

This book is based on the exhibition "School House to White House: The Education of the Presidents," presented at the National Archives, Washington, DC, in the Lawrence F. O'Brien Gallery from March 30, 2007, to January 1, 2008. Over the subsequent two years a traveling version of "School House to White House" is planned to visit Presidential Libraries across the nation.

Library of Congress Cataloging-in-Publication Data

School house to White House : the education of the presidents.
    p. cm.
"Based on an exhibition in the Lawrence F. O'Brien Gallery at the National Archives."
ISBN 978-1-904832-43-0 (hardcover) – ISBN 978-0-9758601-4-4 (softcover)
1. Presidents–Education–United States–Exhibitions. 2. Presidents–United States–Biography–Exhibitions. 3. Presidents–United States–History–20th century Exhibitions. 4. Presidents–United States–History–21st century–Exhibitions. 5. Political leadership–United States–Exhibitions. 6. United States–Politics and government–1929-1933–Exhibitions. 7. United States–Politics and government–1933-1945–Exhibitions. 8. United States–Politics and government–1945-1989–Exhibitions. 9. United States–Politics and government–1989–Exhibitions. I. Foundation for the National Archives.
    E176.1.S3523 2007
    973.09'9--dc22
        2007007372

ISBN (softcover): 978-0-9758601-4-4
ISBN (hardcover): 978-1-904832-43-0

For the Foundation for the National Archives:
Thora Colot, Executive Director
Christina Gehring, Publications and Research Manager

For GILES:
Proofread by Moira Johnston
Designed by Anikst Design, London
Produced by the Publisher, an imprint of D Giles Limited
Printed and bound in China

Photographic Credits
The majority of items reproduced in this book are from the holdings of the National Archives System of Presidential Libraries, which unless otherwise noted, supplied the photographs.

Front cover: Montage of Presidents as schoolchildren. Standing from left to right (back row): Franklin D. Roosevelt, Lyndon B. Johnson, Herbert Hoover, and Ronald Reagan; standing from left to right (front row) George W. Bush, Jimmy Carter, John F. Kennedy, and Dwight D. Eisenhower.

# *Table of Contents*

I am pleased to present *School House to White House: The Education of the Presidents*, a book outlining the educational experiences of our modern Presidents beginning with Herbert Hoover. Here the holdings of the National Archives and Records Administration's (NARA) Presidential Libraries tell a story of scholarship, leadership, and participation in school that helped shape the lives of future Presidents—individuals from diverse backgrounds whose education laid the early groundwork to a range of service in the highest elective office in the land.

This is the story of the education of American leaders although the pages of this book also reveal something else: commonalities between the experiences of young future Presidents and one's own experiences growing and learning in grade school, high school, or college. Just like the rest of us, our modern Presidents were once children and young adults studying, participating in extracurricular activities, and considering career paths. Their story offers important insight into our present situation and raises questions about the education for our future leaders.

Most of the images presented in this book depict documents and artifacts preserved in NARA's Presidential Libraries. These are not typical libraries with books to check out. Rather, these institutions are archives and museums that preserve the written records and physical history of our Presidents while providing special programs and exhibits that serve their communities. They belong to the American people and provide to the public insight into the times in which these Presidents lived and served the nation.

The release of this book coincides with the opening of the exhibit "School House to White House: The Education of the Presidents." The exhibit and book together represent a collaboration among archival and museum staffs of the Presidential Libraries and the Center for the National Archives Experience as well as the support of the Foundation for the National Archives. The exhibit first opened in the National Archives Building in Washington, DC, and then at select Presidential Libraries across the country and includes education and public programs that enhance the visitor's experience. The book, available at NARA gift stores nationwide, will reach many members of the public who have not had the opportunity to visit the exhibit. Coordinating NARA's vast resources in this way supports a significant goal of NARA's strategic plan: increasing access to our records in ways that further civic literacy in America through our museums, public outreach, and education programs.

While attending Stanford as part of the university's first class, Herbert Hoover served as manager of the baseball team and was responsible for collecting admission fees for home games. During one game former President Benjamin Harrison, who was lecturing at Stanford, accidentally gained admission without paying for a ticket. Future-President Hoover caught up with the former President and politely asked for the admission fee which was quickly paid. Hoover said it was "My first contact with a great public man."

Like President Hoover, many of us have had experiences in school that have provided foundations and opportunities for our future lives. Utilizing historical records preserved by the National Archives and its system of Presidential Libraries, this book is an opportunity both to learn about our leaders' educations and to reflect on our own experiences growing up.

Allen Weinstein
Archivist of the United States

# *Acknowledgements*

This book *School House to White House: The Education of the Presidents* and the exhibit upon which it is based were created through a collaboration among the professional archival and museum staffs of the National Archives 12 Presidential Libraries and the Center for the National Archives Experience in Washington, DC, as well as staff from the Office of Presidential Libraries, the National Archives Special Media Preservation Laboratory, and the Foundation for the National Archives.

THE FOLLOWING IS A LIST
OF THESE IMPORTANT
CONTRIBUTORS:

**From the Presidential Libraries:**
Olivia S. Anastasiadis
Karen Anson
Laurie Austin
Kim Barbieri
Clay Bauske
Adam Bergfeld
Mark Beveridge
Steve Branch
Patricia Burchfield
Bonnie Burlbaw
Debbie Carter
Racheal Carter
Stephen Charla
Erik Christman
Bob Clark
Brooke Clement
Josh Cochran
Greg Cumming
Bettina Demetz
Jim Detlefsen
Susan Donius
James Draper
Mike Duggan
Herman Eberhardt
Marcus Ekhardt

Jennifer Evans
Mary Evans
Mary Finch
Michelle Frauenberger
Ray Geselbracht
Renee Gravois
Maryrose Grossman
Marlon Guinn
Ken Hafeli
Elizabeth Hansen
Maureen Harding
Margaret Harman
Nancy Hassett
Kelly Hendren
Donald Holloway
Dan Holt
Spencer Howard
Ben Irwin
John Keller
Sharon Kelly
Tammy Kelly
Cynthia Koch
Michelle Kopfer
James Kratsas
Barbara Kurata
Meghan Lee

Donna Lehman
Jim Leyerzapf
Michael MacDonald
Bill McNitt
Mary Ann McSweeney
Dennis Medina
Christine Mickey
Nancy Mirshah
Tim Morales
Chris Mouw
Nathan Myers
Sylvia Naguib
Audra Oliver
Jay Patton
Jennifer Pedersen
Ira Pemstein
Edward Quick
Mark Renovitch
Scott Roley
Matt Schaefer
Lynn Smith
David Stanhope
Dwight Strandberg
Kathy Struss
Pauline Testerman
Alycia Vivona
Tim Walch
Melissa Walker
Karl Weissenbach
Amy Williams
Ray Wilson

**From the Center for the National Archives Experience:**
Catherine Farmer
Christina Hardman
Karen Hibbitt
Jennifer Nichols Johnson
Darlene McClurkin
Tom Nastick

Marvin Pinkert
Ray Ruskin
Christina Rudy Smith
Maria Stanwich
James Zeender

**From the National Archives Special Media Preservation Laboratory:**
Steve Puglia
Jeffrey Reed

**From the Foundation for the National Archives:**
Bruce Banks
Thora Colot
Franck Cordes
Christina Gehring
Stefanie Mathew
Tibbett Speer

Maureen MacDonald from NARA's Product Development Staff was the exhibit project editor.

The exhibit was coordinated by Jennifer Nichols Johnson and designed by Ray Ruskin. The exhibit script was written by Sharon L. Barry.

Special thanks are extended to Ben Irwin and Christina Gehring for their efforts on the development of this publication.

# *About the Presidential Library System*

The Presidential Library system is made up of 12 Presidential Libraries. This nationwide network of libraries is administered by the Office of Presidential Libraries, which is part of the National Archives and Records Administration (NARA), located in College Park, Maryland. These are not traditional libraries, but rather repositories for preserving and making available the papers, records, and other historical materials of U.S. Presidents since Herbert Hoover. Each Presidential Library contains a museum and provides an active series of education and public programs. When a President leaves office, NARA establishes a Presidential project until a new Presidential Library is built and transferred to the Government.

The Presidential Library system formally began in 1939, when President Franklin Roosevelt donated his personal and Presidential papers to the Federal Government. At the same time, Roosevelt pledged part of his estate at Hyde Park to the United States, and friends of the President formed a nonprofit corporation to raise funds for the construction of the library and museum building. Roosevelt's decision stemmed from a firm belief that Presidential papers are an important part of the national heritage and should be accessible to the public. He asked the National Archives to take custody of his papers and other historical materials and to administer his library. At the dedication of his library on June 30, 1941, Franklin Roosevelt observed:

*To bring together the records of the past and to house them in buildings where they will be preserved for the use of men and women in the future, a Nation must believe in three things.*

*It must believe in the past.*
*It must believe in the future.*
*It must, above all, believe in the capacity of its own people so to learn from the past that they can gain in judgment in creating their own future.*

THE NATIONAL ARCHIVES
PRESIDENTIAL LIBRARIES

Office of Presidential Libraries
National Archives at College Park
8601 Adelphi Road
College Park, MD 20740-6001
301-837-3250
F: 301-837-3199
W: www.archives.gov/presidential-libraries/

Herbert Hoover Presidential Library
210 Parkside Drive, P.O. Box 488
West Branch, IA 52358-0488
319-643-5301
F: 319-643-6045
E: hoover.library@nara.gov
W: http://hoover.archives.gov

Franklin D. Roosevelt Presidential Library
4079 Albany Post Road
Hyde Park, NY 12538-1999
1-800-FDR-VISIT or 845-486-7770
F: 845-486-1147
E: roosevelt.library@nara.gov
W: www.fdrlibrary.marist.edu

Harry S. Truman Presidential Library
500 West U.S. Highway 24
Independence, MO 64050-1798
816-268-8200
F: 816-268-8295
E: truman.library@nara.gov
W: www.trumanlibrary.org

Dwight D. Eisenhower Presidential Library
200 Southeast Fourth Street
Abilene, KS 67410-2900
785-263-4751
F: 785-263-6718
E: eisenhower.library@nara.gov
W: www.eisenhower.archives.gov

John Fitzgerald Kennedy Presidential Library
Columbia Point
Boston, MA 02125-3398
877-616-4599 (toll free) or 617-514-1600
F: 617-514-1652
E: kennedy.library@nara.gov
W: www.jfklibrary.org

Lyndon Baines Johnson Presidential Library
2313 Red River Street
Austin, TX 78705-5702
512-721-0200
F: 512-721-0170
E: johnson.library@nara.gov
W: www.lbjlib.utexas.edu

Richard Nixon Presidential Library
18001 Yorba Linda Boulevard
Yorba Linda, CA 92886
714-983-9120
F: 714-983-9111
E: nixon@nara.gov
W: www.nixon.archives.gov

Gerald R. Ford Presidential Library and Museum

Gerald R. Ford Library
1000 Beal Avenue
Ann Arbor, MI 48109-2114
734-205-0555
F: 734-205-0571
E: ford.library@nara.gov
W: www.fordlibrarymuseum.gov

Gerald R. Ford Museum
303 Pearl Street, NW
Grand Rapids, MI 49504-5353
616-254-0400
F: 616-254-0386
E: ford.museum@nara.gov
W: www.fordlibrarymuseum.gov

Jimmy Carter Presidential Library
441 Freedom Parkway
Atlanta, GA 30307-1498
404-865-7100
F: 404-865-7102
E: carterlibrary@nara.gov
W: www.jimmycarterlibrary.gov

Ronald Reagan Presidential Library
40 Presidential Drive
Simi Valley, CA 93065-0699
800-410-8354 or 805-577-4000
F: 805-577-4074
E: reagan.library@nara.gov
W: www.reagan.utexas.edu

George H.W. Bush Presidential Library
1000 George Bush Drive, West
College Station, TX 77845
979-691-4000
F: 979-691-4050
E: bush.library@nara.gov
W: www.bushlibrary.tamu.edu

William J. Clinton Presidential Library
1200 President Clinton Avenue
Little Rock, AR 72201
501-244-2887
F: 501-244-2883
E: clinton.library@nara.gov
W: www.clinton.library.gov

Presidential Materials Staff
National Archives and Records Administration
700 Pennsylvania Avenue, NW
Washington, DC 20408-0001
202-357-5200
F: 202-357-5939

# *Introduction*

In 230 years, fewer than 45 people have become President of the United States. Before achieving the highest office in the land, each of these exceptional Americans was once a boy struggling with his studies, a teenager trying to fit in, and a young man choosing a career path. Like many Americans, Presidents once competed for a spot on the football team or a place in their school's band. The challenges of studying various subjects, completing homework, forming new ideas, participating in extracurricular activities, and making friends are part of the common heritage of an American education shared by everyone—including our Presidents.

This book presents the story of the education of the 20th-century Presidents by exploring the holdings of the National Archives system of Presidential Libraries—documents, artifacts, and photographs kept for each President from Herbert Hoover to Bill Clinton. These are not libraries in the usual sense, but rather archives and museums that bring together in one place the materials of a President and his administration and present them to the public for study and discussion without regard for political considerations or affiliations. President Ronald Reagan once described Presidential Libraries as "classrooms of democracy." Here, the holdings of the Libraries illustrate what our leaders accomplished in the classrooms of their youth.

These modern Presidents came from diverse backgrounds, and their educations reflect these differences. Some of the Presidents attended neighborhood public schools, and some of them learned in rural classrooms; others studied under tutors and attended prestigious private schools. Many of the Presidents participated in extracurricular activities and organized sports while they attended school. Although the Presidents examined in this book were good students, an occasional poor grade did appear on a report card. As it is for most of us, education in school and related activities were influential to future Presidents and provided a foundation on which they built the rest of their lives.

This book is an invitation to explore Presidential schooldays through the collections of the National Archives system of Presidential Libraries. Learning about our leaders' lives in school provides for new connections to and perspectives on the Presidency and those who have served as President. It is also an opportunity to reflect on one's own experiences growing up and learning about the world. The school bell is ringing, and everyone has a desk. It's time to go back to school. The Presidents are expecting you.

# Home

"*My mother read these to me before
I could read, but I took keen joy
in them for many later years.*"

*Franklin D. Roosevelt's*
*inscription in a companion volume*

*below*
**The Great Panjandrum Himself by**
**Samuel Foote**
*Franklin D. Roosevelt Presidential*
*Library and Museum*

*right*
**Jimmy Carter playing with his pony, Lady Lee, ca. 1931**
*Jimmy Carter Presidential Library and Museum*

*middle*
**Franklin D. Roosevelt, about 14 years old, Germany, 1896**
*Franklin D. Roosevelt Presidential Library and Museum*

*bottom*
**Herbert Hoover (center) with his brother Theodore and sister Mary, West Branch, Iowa, ca. 1881**
*Herbert Hoover Presidential Library and Museum*

For the Presidents, success in school began at home. Whether having stories read to them before bed or checking out books from the library over the summer, these young men grew up in homes that furthered their education. Their parents were often supportive, providing opportunities to learn and an environment to explore interests. For example, Franklin Roosevelt's mother, Sara Delano Roosevelt, closely supervised his education. In addition to arranging for tutors, taking him on educational trips abroad, and encouraging his collecting hobbies, Sara read regularly to young Franklin. *The Great Panjandrum Himself* by Samuel Foote, a popular 18th-century nonsense story, and other children's books are part of Roosevelt's personal book collection of some 17,000 volumes at the Roosevelt Library.

*above*
***Idylls of the King* by
Alfred, Lord Tennyson**
*Harry S. Truman
Presidential Library and
Museum*

Authors treasured in high school could emerge to impact the President later in life. In April 1901, 16-year-old Harry Truman bought *Idylls of the King* by Alfred, Lord Tennyson. He marked a passage in which a knight tells his mother that he's now a man and must find his destiny. " 'Follow the Christ, the King,' " he says. " 'Live pure, speak true, right wrong, follow the King. / Else, wherefore born?' " Attracted to Tennyson's broad idealism, Truman always carried a handwritten fragment of Tennyson's poem, "Locksley Hall."

Jimmy Carter wrote in his autobiography, "My life was heavily influenced by our school superintendent, Miss Julia Coleman, who encouraged me to learn about music, art, and especially literature.... She encouraged all of her students to seek cultural knowledge beyond the requirements of a normal rural school classroom." Miss Coleman obtained a one-year grant from the Works Progress Administration (WPA) in 1940 to keep the library open for the summer and used the slogan "Readers Make Leaders" to encourage reading.

The home also provided a place to practice new activities. Richard Nixon learned to play the violin, clarinet, saxophone, piano, and the accordion. When he was 12, Richard was sent to live and study music with his mother's sister in central California for six months. His love of music continued throughout his life.

*left*
**Richard Nixon, age 15, holding his violin, 1928**
*Records of the U.S. Information Agency, National Archives, Courtesy of AP/ Wide World Photos*

*below*
**Wood violin**
*Courtesy of the Richard Nixon Library and Birthplace*

*left*
**"Readers Make Leaders" certificate, Plains Public School, June 3, 1940**
*Jimmy Carter Presidential Library and Museum*

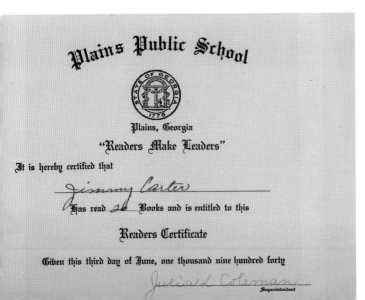

Plains Public School

Plains, Georgia

"Readers Make Leaders"

It is hereby certified that

Jimmy Carter

Has read 26 Books and is entitled to this

Readers Certificate

Given this third day of June, one thousand nine hundred forty

Julia L. Coleman
Superintendent

# *Home*

*left*

**George H.W. Bush, approximately age 12, ca. 1936**
*George H.W. Bush Presidential Library and Museum*

*below*

**Lyndon B. Johnson (in front of the automobile), age 4, and his family, near Stonewall, Texas, ca. 1912**
*Lyndon Baines Johnson Presidential Library and Museum*

*above*
**Harry S. Truman (second from left) and members of his family in a farm wagon, Grandview, Missouri, ca. 1911**
*Harry S. Truman Presidential Library and Museum*

*left*
**Gerald R. Ford, on bike, with cousin Gardner James (left) and two unidentified girls in front of his first home, 1960 Terrace, in Grand Rapids, Michigan, ca. 1915**
*Gerald R. Ford Presidential Library and Museum*

# Grade School

*"In grammar school, spelling was probably my favorite subject either because the contest aroused my competitive instincts or because I had learned that a single letter could make a vast difference in the meaning of a word."*

Dwight D. Eisenhower

*left*
**Jimmy Carter's sixth grade report card, Plains High School, Plains, Georgia, 1935–36**
*Jimmy Carter Presidential Library and Museum*

*below*
**Jimmy Carter's fourth grade geography test, Plains High School, Plains, Georgia, ca. 1933**
*Jimmy Carter Presidential Library and Museum*

From their very first day of school, whether in a one-room schoolhouse, neighborhood school, or a private academy, the future Presidents discovered a new, larger world full of facts, figures, and ideas. Many Presidents learned lessons from their teachers that they would remember for the rest of their lives. While in school, a few future Presidents had to overcome the extraordinary challenges of illness, poverty, or the deaths of parents or siblings. Whether their experiences were reflective of their times and communities or were universal to American schooling, they helped mold the characters of these boys who grew up to be President.

**Ronald Reagan (second row, far left, with hand on his chin), fourth grade class photo, Tampico, Illinois, 1920**
*Ronald Reagan Presidential Library and Museum*

# Grade School

*left*
**Dwight D. Eisenhower (front row, second from left), fifth grade class, Lincoln Elementary School, Abilene, Kansas, 1900**
*Dwight D. Eisenhower Presidential Library and Museum*

About his years in school, Dwight Eisenhower later wrote: "At one point a suggestion was made that I should 'skip' a grade. This is not tribute to any academic mastery. I suspect that it was simply recognition that I lived in a home where learning was put into practice.... The suggestion that I skip a grade was never put into effect. My conduct was not the equal of my reading ability."

*above*
**Herbert Hoover (front row, far right side) with classmates, about 11 years old, Oregon, 1885**
*Herbert Hoover Presidential Library and Museum*

Harry Truman's only surviving report card has puzzled his biographers. His teacher wrote on the card that it was for second grade, but Truman later remembered that he was in fourth grade this year.

They were probably both right. The report card indicates he started the 1894–95 year in class "A," which was the third term of second grade. He probably skipped a term, or possibly two terms, and by year's end was in the fourth grade.

An example of Harry Truman's homework is "Courage" (1899), an essay from his eighth grade English theme book. He wrote this essay when he was about 15 years old. In it he states a preference for a quiet kind of courage to the more traditional active heroism. He concludes his essay with an outburst of idealism: "A true heart[,] a strong mind[,] and a great deal of courage and I think a man will get through the world."

*above*
**Harry S. Truman's second grade report card, Columbian School, Independence, Missouri, 1894**
*Harry S. Truman Presidential Library and Museum*

*below*
**"Courage," an essay from Harry S. Truman's eighth grade English book.**
*Courtesy of Martha Ann Swoyer*

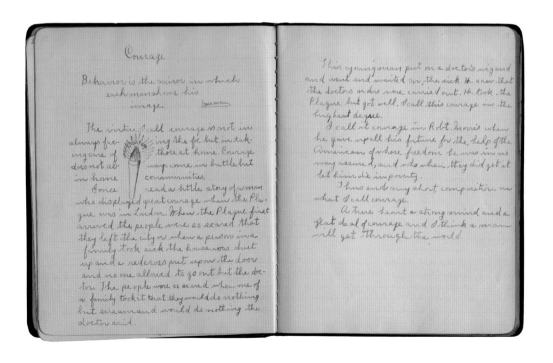

## *Grade School*

As with Truman, writing was an important part of these future Presidents' learning experience. For example, shortly after the death of his younger brother Arthur, Richard Nixon wrote an autobiographical essay about his childhood and his ambitions for the future. In it he wrote, "One of the things that made an impression on me was the death of my younger brother Arthur." Richard continued writing: "He was very well liked by everybody [,] having a happy spirit."

*above*
**Richard Nixon (far right, first row), first grade, Yorba Linda, California, 1919**
*Courtesy of the Richard Nixon Library and Birthplace*

Richard Nixon.      Oct 29 1925
East Whittier      Eighth Grade

Autobiography

I was born on January the ninth, nineteen thirteen in the town of Yorba Linda California. The house that I was born in was a big two story building situated in the southwest part of town. It had a large fire place in it. An irrigation canal that was used in watering the nearby ranches ran close by the house. The ranch of about fourteen acres consisted of lemons, oranges, and deciduous trees such as apples, pears, plums, peaches, apricots. And a few others.

One of the times of the year that I looked forward to was the time that that the over crop was sown and had reached its full hieght over night.

from our old home to East Whittier. It was a very big change but I liked it very much.

I have attended three schools Yorba Linda, Sunnyside, and East Whittier. In my first four years I went to Yorba Linda School. My next three years and a half I went to East Whittier. In the last six months of my seventh year I went to a another school between and Bakersfield. I then started the eighth year at East Whittier. The subjects that I enjoyed the most are History and Geography. I also like debate. One of my best chums at school was a boy named Paul Herbert. We had some fine times together.

One event that made an impression on me was the death of my youngest

brother Arthur. He was born in nineteen eighteen at Yorba Linda. He was seven years old when he died. He was very well liked by everybody having a happy spirit. The cause of his death is not known but it is generally considered that it was caused by tuberculosis of the brain.

One of the things that I like to do better than anything else is to read a good book, magazine or a paper. I also like music pretty well.

My plans for the future are to finish Whittier high school and also to take postgraduate work at Columbia University New York. I would also like to visit Europe. I would like to study law and enter politics for an occupation so that I might be of some good to the people.

*above and left*
**Richard Nixon's school paper, "Autobiography," written in eighth grade, 1925, title page, pages 3 and 4**
*Courtesy of the Richard Nixon Library and Birthplace*

# Grade School

John F. Kennedy, second of nine children, was born on Beals Street, a block away from Edward Devotion School. John attended Edward Devotion when he was about four years old. Rose Kennedy noted the health of her children on cards and on John's card his mother listed some of his childhood diseases. His Edward Devotion school records show that John was present only 23 days out of the 88-day term.

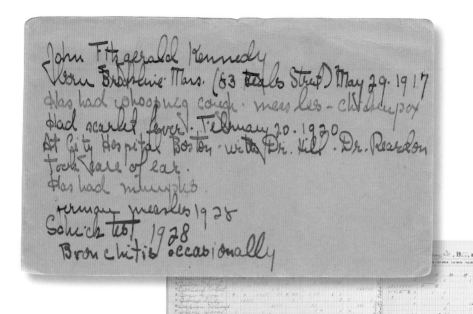

*above*
**Health records of John F. Kennedy, written by his mother, Rose Kennedy, 1917–28**
*John F. Kennedy Presidential Library and Museum*

*right*
**John F. Kennedy's kindergarten attendance records, Edward Devotion School, Brookline, Massachusetts, 1922**
*John F. Kennedy Presidential Library and Museum*

## CANTERBURY SCHOOL
### NEW MILFORD, CONNECTICUT

Record of John Kennedy, Form II

From November 1 to December 6, 1930.

Any average from 90% to 100% is accounted "Very Good"; from 80% to 90% "Good"; from 70% to 80% "Fair"; from 60% to 70% "Poor"; and below 60% "Unsatisfactory".

| SUBJECT | DAILY WORK | EFFORT AND APPLICATION | FORM AVERAGE |
|---------|------------|------------------------|--------------|
| English II | 86 | Good | 71.69 |
| Latin II | 55 | Poor | 64.35 |
| History II | 77 | Good | 67.00 |
| Mathematics II | 95 | Good | 61.69 |
| Science II | 72 | Good | 66.62 |
| Religion II | 75 | Fair | 78.46 |
| AVERAGE: 77.00 | | | |

This report is not quite so good as the last one. The damage was done chiefly by "Poor" effort in Latin, in which Jack got a mark of 55. He can do better than this. In fact, his average should be well in the 80's.

N.H.

*above*
**John F. Kennedy (sitting in the middle of the first row), Riverdale Country Day School, Bronxville, New York, ca. 1927–28**
*Photograph by Arthur Studios, John F. Kennedy Library and Museum*

*right*
**John F. Kennedy's report card, Canterbury School, New Milford, Connecticut, December 1930**
*John F. Kennedy Presidential Library and Museum*

Rose and Joseph Kennedy enrolled their son John at Canterbury School from 1930–31, an exclusive Catholic Academy in Milford, Connecticut. While there, John wrote a report on Francis the First. The first page is written in French.

*above and right*
**"Francis the First,"
written by John F.
Kennedy, ca. 1930, pages
1, 9, 10**
*John F. Kennedy Presidential
Library and Museum*

Rebekah Johnson taught her son Lyndon the alphabet by the age of three. At four he could read and followed his cousins to the local elementary school to sit in on the classes. Lyndon began his formal schooling in first grade when he attended the Johnson City School.

*above*
**Lyndon B. Johnson's third grade report card, Johnson City, Texas, 1917**
*Courtesy of the Collection of Johnson City Foundation*

*Grade School*

After George H.W. Bush graduated from Yale, he moved his family to Texas. His oldest child, George W. Bush, was three years old when they moved.

*above*

**Gerald R. Ford, Madison Elementary School, Grand Rapids, Michigan, ca. 1923**
*Gerald R. Ford Presidential Library and Museum*

*above*

**George W. Bush with his father George H.W. Bush, March 20, 1956**
*George H.W. Bush Presidential Library and Museum*

*right*

**George W. Bush's first grade report card, Sam Houston Elementary School, Midland, Texas, 1952–53**
*George H.W. Bush Presidential Library and Museum*

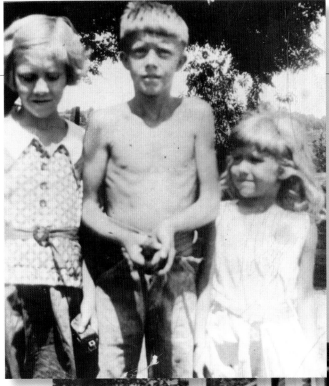

Jimmy Carter grew up in rural Georgia in the 1930s and attended the same school, Plains High School, from 1st through 11th grade.

*left*
**Jimmy Carter, around 10 years old, with his sisters Gloria, age 8, and Ruth, age 5**
*Jimmy Carter Presidential Library and Museum*

*above*
**Bill Clinton (far left) at Miss Mary's Kindergarten, Hope, Arkansas, May 6, 1950**
*Courtesy of William J. Clinton*

# High School

*"In my childhood a high school education was an exceptional opportunity for an American boy or girl; a college education was possible only to an exceedingly small minority."*

*Franklin D. Roosevelt*

*above*
**Gerald R. Ford's high school record card, South High School, Grand Rapids, Michigan, June 19, 1931**
*Gerald R. Ford Presidential Library and Museum*

High school is an important time for students as they make their transition from child to young adult in a setting of expanding educational and extracurricular experiences. After grade school, some future Presidents attended their local high school, while others went away to boarding school. As their classwork became more varied and demanding, their report cards reveal how well they succeeded with these more challenging courses. Whether their school was large or small, a little-known public school or a well-known private academy, each young man's world of education, sports, and social activities expanded in high school.

*left*
**Harry S. Truman (top row, fourth from the left), senior class, Independence High School, Independence, Missouri, ca. 1901**
*Harry S. Truman Presidential Library and Museum*

*above*
**Dwight D. Eisenhower's high school transcript, Abilene High School, Abilene, Kansas, 1905–09**
*Courtesy of the Dickenson County Historical Society*

Until the age of 14, Franklin Roosevelt was taught by private tutors. When he entered school at Groton, a private academy for the privileged in Massachusetts, it was his first time away from his parents and one of his first experiences in a classroom with other students. At Groton, Franklin met one of his lifelong role models, Endicott Peabody, founder and longtime headmaster of the Groton School.

28-39

*Franklin's first report*

## GROTON SCHOOL,
### GROTON, MASS.

Report of *F. Roosevelt III Form*

for the month ending *Oct 17 - 1896*

Rank in Class of *19* Boys *4*

| | | MONTHLY AVERAGE. | EXAMINATION MARKS. |
|---|---|---|---|
| Latin, | | 7.70 | |
| | Composition, | 6.75 | |
| Greek, | | | |
| | Composition, | | |
| | Trigonometry, | | |
| Mathematics, | Geometry, | | |
| | Algebra, | 9.75 | |
| | Arithmetic, | | |
| | Literature, | 8.50 | |
| English, | Composition, | 8.40 | |
| | Grammar, | | |
| | Reading, | | |
| French, | | 8.00 | |
| German, | | | |
| History, | | 7.33 | |
| Science, | | 7.50 | |
| Physics, | | | |
| Sacred Studies, | | 8.00 | |
| Punctuality, | | 10.00 | |
| Neatness, | | 9.68 | |
| Decorum, | | | |
| AVERAGE MARK FOR THE MONTH, | | 7.79 | |
| AVERAGE MARK FOR THE TERM, | | | |

REMARKS. *Very good. He strikes me as an intelligent & faithful scholar & a good boy.*

*E. Peabody*

*above*
**Franklin D. Roosevelt's formal portrait, Groton School, 1900**
*Franklin D. Roosevelt Presidential Library and Museum*

*left*
**Franklin D. Roosevelt's Groton School report card, Groton, Massachusetts, October 1896**
*Franklin D. Roosevelt Presidential Library and Museum*

deal and I have gained several pounds.

I am going to Groton on Wednesday for the second time. A number of boys have fruit sent them and it is kept in the fruit closet and given out three or four times a week. Could you send me some grapes or other small fruit? It would be very nice.

With lots of love to Muriel and Warren and papa and yourself

affectionately

Franklin D Roosevelt

Groton School
Sept. 27th '96

Dear Papa and Mama

I am getting on very well so far. Thanks very much for your letters; the more the better.

I have not had any blackmarks or latenesses yet and I am much better in my studies.

I got the best mark in Algebra yesterday this morning and the day before I got the best in English Composition. Yesterday

afternoon our 1st Eleven we played the Brookline High School team, a lot of toughs, and beat them quite badly, the score was 16 – 0 and for the first game of the season it was very good.

I cheered myself hoarse so that I was quite croaky at choir practice.

I like Greek very much, it is very easy so far, and Mr. Abbott, a young Englishman just come to the school, gives us very short lessons. I am going to try for the punctuality

prize, but it will be hard work, as one lateness will spoil.

The Biddle boy is quite crazy, fresh and stupid, he has been boot-boxed once and threatened to be pumped several times. Our 4th twenty-two play four times a week, and we have had some very desperate battles. My head is a little bunged up, but otherwise I am all right. Mr. Peabody read to us in his study several evenings in the week after supper. I eat a great

Roosevelt, who wrote home daily, had been at Groton for less than a month when he reported, "I have not had any blackmarks or latenesses yet."

**Franklin D. Roosevelt's letter home to parents while at Groton, September 27, 1896**
*Franklin D. Roosevelt Presidential Library and Museum*

As an adult, Dwight Eisenhower reflected on his education: "In the fall of 1896, I entered the Lincoln School, little aware that I was starting on a road in formal education which would not terminate until 1929 when I finished courses at the Army's War College in Washington, DC. What I learned at the start would not remain static. In the third of a century between my first and last school was compressed a series of revolutions—political and economic, social and scientific—which were to transform the human environment of the entire globe."

*above*
**Dwight D. Eisenhower (back row, far left), freshman class, Abilene High School, Abilene, Kansas, 1905**
*Dwight D. Eisenhower Presidential Library and Museum*

*above*

**Dwight D. Eisenhower's high school portrait, Abilene High School, Abilene, Kansas, 1909**
*Dwight D. Eisenhower Presidential Library and Museum*

Fifth Annual
National Oratorical Contest
On the Constitution

Orange County
District Six
Brea-Olinda Union High School
March 30, 1928

Program for the Evening Conducted by
PI SIGMA KAPPA
(Public Speaking Club)

THIS year marks the Fifth Annual National Oratorical Contest on the Constitution. Its value from the standpoint of interest in our government, as well as in public speaking, cannot be over-estimated. The district in which this contest is held feels a debt of gratitude to the Los Angeles Times for all that it has done in sponsoring and promoting this

Contestants will draw for their places just before the program begins.

**JUDGES**
(Selected by the Los Angeles Times)

EMERSON SEAR,
General Manager, Pacific Wire Products Co.

A R. WALKER,
Debate Coach, Alhambra High School

F. O. D. WOOD,
Formerly President of the Lucknow Christian College, India.

**Programme**

Chairman, Principal I. W. Barnett

Quartette { Pale in the Amber West—Parks
The World is Waiting for the Sunrise—Sietz
William Collins, Melvin McMechan,
Clarence Wise, Adelbert Fiscus

GENERAL TOPIC: "THE DEVELOPMENT OR THE SIGNIFICANCE OF THE CONSTITUTION"

"THE EVER-INCREASING STRENGTH OF THE CONSTITUTION"—Richard Nixon, Fullerton

"THE IDEALS OF THE CONSTITUTION"
Martha Spaulding, Santa Ana

"THE LIVING CONSTITUTION"
Thomas Russell, Anaheim

"THE MODERN SIGNIFICANCE OF THE CONSTITUTION"
Evelyn Parks, Garden Grove

"SOURCES OF THE CONSTITUTION"
Isabel Siracusa, Huntington Beach

"THE DEVELOPMENT OF THE CONSTITUTION"
Winifred Barnett, Brea-Olinda

"THE RELATIONSHIP BETWEEN THE INDIVIDUAL AND THE CONSTITUTION"—Earl Lyon, Orange

Pale Moon ............................................ Logan
Out of the Dusk to You ............................ Lee
Lucile Coggeshall, Mary Hunt, Gwen Pendleton Shaffer,
Nondys Smith, Ethel Peak, Jane Bernett, Georgia Grant,
Laura Merrifield.

Richard Nixon, described as a shy, quiet student, was the Constitutional Oratorical Champion in 1928, 1929, and 1930. He graduated first in his class with honors from Whittier Union High School in 1930.

**Program for an oratorical contest, March 30, 1928**
*Courtesy of the Richard Nixon Library and Birthplace*

# High school

Gerald Ford was named a member of the National Honor Society in high school, an award that honored students who excelled in both academics and athletics.

*left*
**Gerald R. Ford's graduation portrait, South High School, Michigan, 1931**
*Gerald R. Ford Presidential Library and Museum*

*left*
**Jimmy Carter (on left, holding flag) with Future Farmers of America club, ca. 1940**
*Jimmy Carter Presidential Library and Museum*

*left*

**Lyndon B. Johnson's ninth grade report card, Johnson City High School, Johnson City, Texas, 1921–22**
*Courtesy of the Collection of Johnson City Foundation*

*below*

**Lyndon B. Johnson (back row, fifth from left), Johnson City High School, Johnson City, Texas, 1924**
*Lyndon Baines Johnson Presidential Library and Museum*

# High School

Theme
Ronald Reagan
English II
Nov. 6 - 1925

$10.50

Hallowe'en

'Twas the nite of Hallowe'en, but nothing was still. The good people went to sleep that memorable Saturday night with the sounds of laughter, running feet, and muffled shouts ringing in their ears. Then were they peaceful, and only then, for at twelve o'clock a gasping, panting roar awakened the town. The north bound passenger was waiting on the siding. The freight due from the north was vainly fighting to get over a hundred foot stretch of greased track. These trains were only held a mere matter of an hour and a half by the exuberance of a striving juvenile populace.

But the next morning a greater shock came. The city was transformed, but less beautiful. The telephone poles were artistically draped with porch furniture, signs, and various parts of buggies and wagons. The streets looked like rummage sales while schools and stores found their doorways filled with representatives of the last night's toil.

But alas! Except for an occasional chair on a telephone pole, the scene was soon shattered by the respective owners of the collected articles.

B+

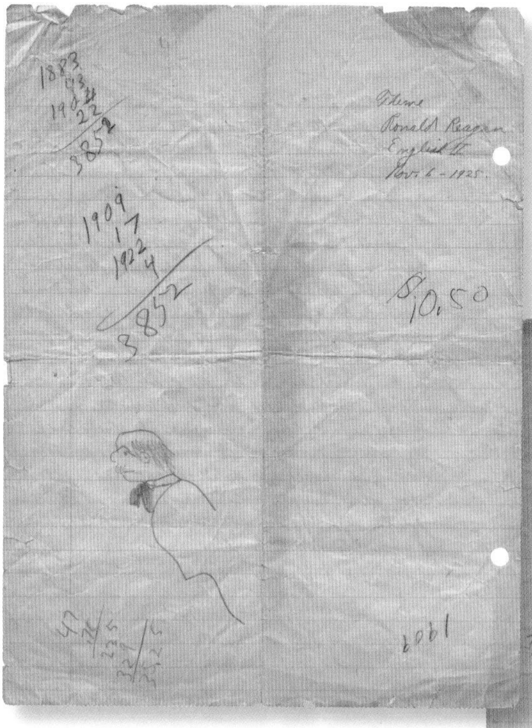

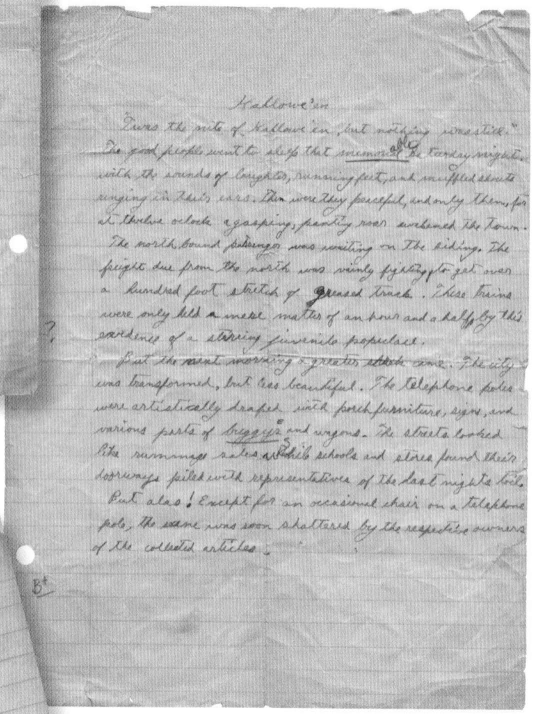

*left and below*
**Essay, "Hallowe'en," written by Ronald Reagan, Dixon High School, Dixon, Illinois, ca. 1925**
*Ronald Reagan Presidential Library and Museum*

French 4.
Morris Coleridge
William Austin.
Rushville, Ill.

presse – hurry
le sang – blood
la sagesse – wisdom
les agneaux – lambs
une échelle – ladder
la farine – flour
la poussière – powder, dust.
sauver – to save
les minoteries – steam mills
virer – turn, revolve, whirl.
sangloter – to get angry
s'entasser – to crush
tandis que – while
s'envoler – to cover
le froment – wheat

*left*
**Ronald Reagan's French exam, Dixon High School, Dixon, Illinois, ca. 1925**
*Ronald Reagan Presidential Library and Museum*

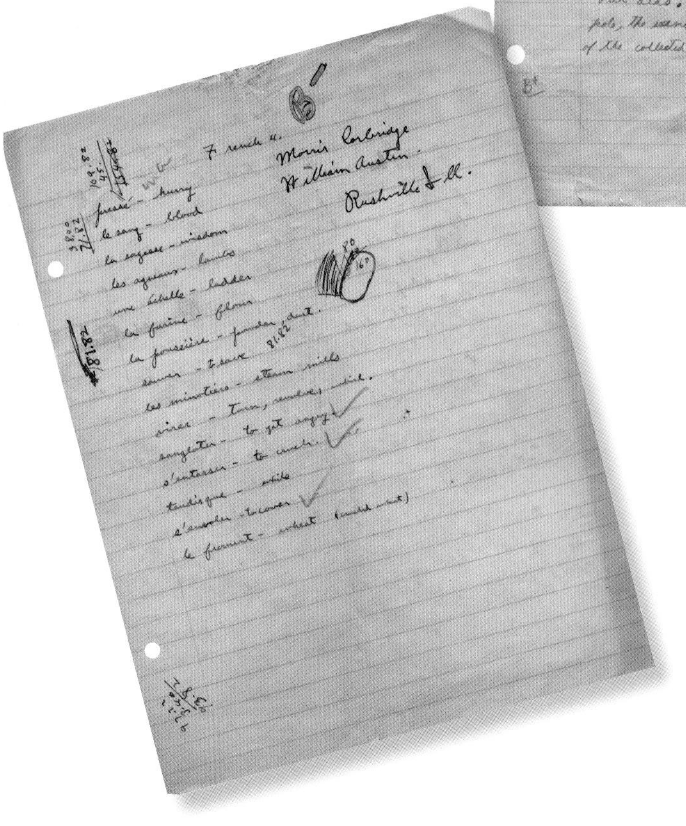

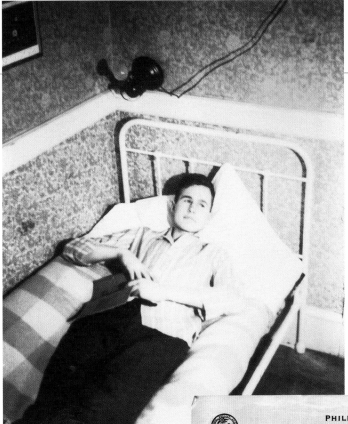

*left*

**George H.W. Bush in his bed at Phillips Academy, Andover, Massachusetts, unknown date**
*George H.W. Bush Presidential Library and Museum*

*below*

**George H.W. Bush's final transcript, Phillips Academy, Andover, Massachusetts, May 26, 1942**
*George H.W. Bush Presidential Library and Museum*

George H.W. Bush attended Phillips Academy, one of the best private schools in the country, in Andover, Massachusetts. On June 12, 1942, just months after the United States entered World War II, George graduated from Phillips. That day he enlisted in the U.S. Navy.

## PHILLIPS ACADEMY
### ANDOVER, MASSACHUSETTS
RECORDER'S OFFICE

THIS IS TO CERTIFY THAT George Herbert Walker Bush has been a member of this school from Sept. 1937 to date and that the record of his work while in attendance is given below.

Number of weeks of actual instruction in each year, 35. Actual length of the class period, 53 minutes. A double laboratory period is called equivalent to a single recitation period.

The passing mark is 60 and the honor marks are 80 and above.
Grades in brackets, as (70), are approximate for the work done in courses which the student did not complete.
Accredited by New England College Entrance Certificate Board.

| COURSE | YEAR | PERIODS A WEEK | GRADE | COURSE | YEAR | PERIODS A WEEK | GRADE |
|---|---|---|---|---|---|---|---|
| English 1 | 1937-38 | 4 | 75 | Mathematics 1 | 1937-38 | 5 | 70 |
| 2 | 1938-39 | 3 | 75 | Mathematics 2 | 1938-39 | 4 | 75 |
| 2 (Oral) | 1938-39 | 1 | 70 | Mathematics 3 (Beta) * | 1939-40 | 4 | 75 55 |
| 3 | 1939-40 | 3 | 60 | Mathematics 4 (Gamma) | | | |
| 4 | 1940-41 | 4 | 73 | Mathematics 6 3(Beta) | 1940-41 | 4 | 68 |
| 5 Fall Term | 1941-42 | 3 | 72 | Mathematics 7 | | | |
| Public Speaking | | | | Mechanical Drawing | 1940-41 | 2 | 71 Fall & Winter |
| French 1 | 1937-38 | 4 | 71 | Elementary Science | 1938-39 | 2 | 75 |
| 2 | 1938-39 | 4 | 68 | Biology * | 1939-40 | 4 | 71 70 |
| 3 | 1939-40 | 4 | 64 | Chemistry | 1940-41 | 4 | 55 |
| 4 | 1940-41 | 4 | 62 | ~~Physics~~ Chemistry # | 1941-42 | 3 | 77 86 |
| | | | | Anthropology | | | |
| German 1-2 ** # | 1941-42 | 5 | 76 80 | Art, Studio | 1939-40 | 2 | 60 |
| 2 | | | | Music, Introduction to | | | |
| 3 | | | | Music | | | |
| 4 | | | | Astronomy | | | |
| Greek 1 | | | | Philosophy | | | |
| 2 | | | | Religion | 1938-39 | 2 | 78 |
| 3 | | | | Social Problems | | | |
| 4 | | | | Anatomy & Evolution | 1941-42 | 2 | 70 Fall Term |
| Latin 1 | 1937-38 | 5 | 65 | | | | |
| 2 | 1937-38 | 4 | 60 | Communications ## | 1941-42 | 1 | 70 |
| 3 | 1938-39 | 5 | 70 | Mathematics S ## | 1941-42 | 4 | (75) |
| 4 | | | | | | | |
| Spanish 1 | | | | *Fall and Winter Terms - ill from April 14 to | | | |
| 2 | | | | June 13, 1940. | | | |
| History Ancient | 1937-38 | 3 | 70 | **Two years completed in one year. | | | |
| European | | | | ##Began during Winter Term - will be completed | | | |
| English * | 1939-40 | 3 | 70 75 | June 12, 1942 | | | |
| American # | 1941-42 | 5 | 73 81 | | | | |
| English | 1940-41 | 3 | 77 Spring Term | | | | |

#Fall & Winter Terms - will be completed June 12, 1942

Date of Graduation ............... Position in his Class for year ...... Fall Term 59 Winter Term ... Number in the Class ...... 214 213

Date May 26, 1942

Signature *Alice T. Whitney*
Recorder

# College

"*Everything that has been good in my life began here*"

*Ronald Reagan*

The 20th-century Presidents grew up in a time when fewer people attended college than today. All of them went to college in some form, from small institution or night school to law school or a service academy. For many of them, college was an extraordinary opportunity and a major step forward in their lives and in their future public service. Just like many students experience today, college was a place where the future Presidents made lifelong friends and started down paths that would lead to important career choices.

# College

In 1891, Herbert Hoover was a member of the first class of the newly established Stanford University, where he studied geology. His college experience gave him important training which he would later use to become a successful mining engineer.

*above*
**Stanford University surveying squad. Herbert Hoover is on the bottom left, 1893**
*Herbert Hoover Presidential Library and Museum*

*above*
**Photograph taken at the inauguration of President Woodrow Wilson. Eisenhower is sixth from the right in the front row, 1913**
*Dwight D. Eisenhower Presidential Library and Museum*

*right*
**Dwight D. Eisenhower's formal cadet portrait, West Point, 1915**
*Dwight D. Eisenhower Presidential Library and Museum*

Dwight Eisenhower attended West Point. As an adult, he remembered his family's emphasis on education: "From the beginning of our schooling, Mother and Father encouraged us [Eisenhower boys] to go to college. They said constantly, 'Anyone who really wants an education can get it.' But my father, remembering that he didn't become a farmer as his father had hoped, scrupulously refrained from suggesting courses of study."

*College*

*left and below*
**John F. Kennedy's class
notes, Government I,
Harvard University,
Cambridge, Massachusetts,
1937–38**
*John F. Kennedy Presidential
Library and Museum*

*right*
**John F. Kennedy's Harvard
transcript, Cambridge,
Massachusetts, 1939–40**
*John F. Kennedy Presidential
Library and Museum*

THIS BOOK BELONGS TO

John F. Kennedy
Winthrop J-23

CLASS OF 1940

Government I

HARVARD COÖPERATIVE SOCIETY
· · · *JOIN THE COÖP* · · ·
COÖP PURCHASES PAY DIVIDENDS

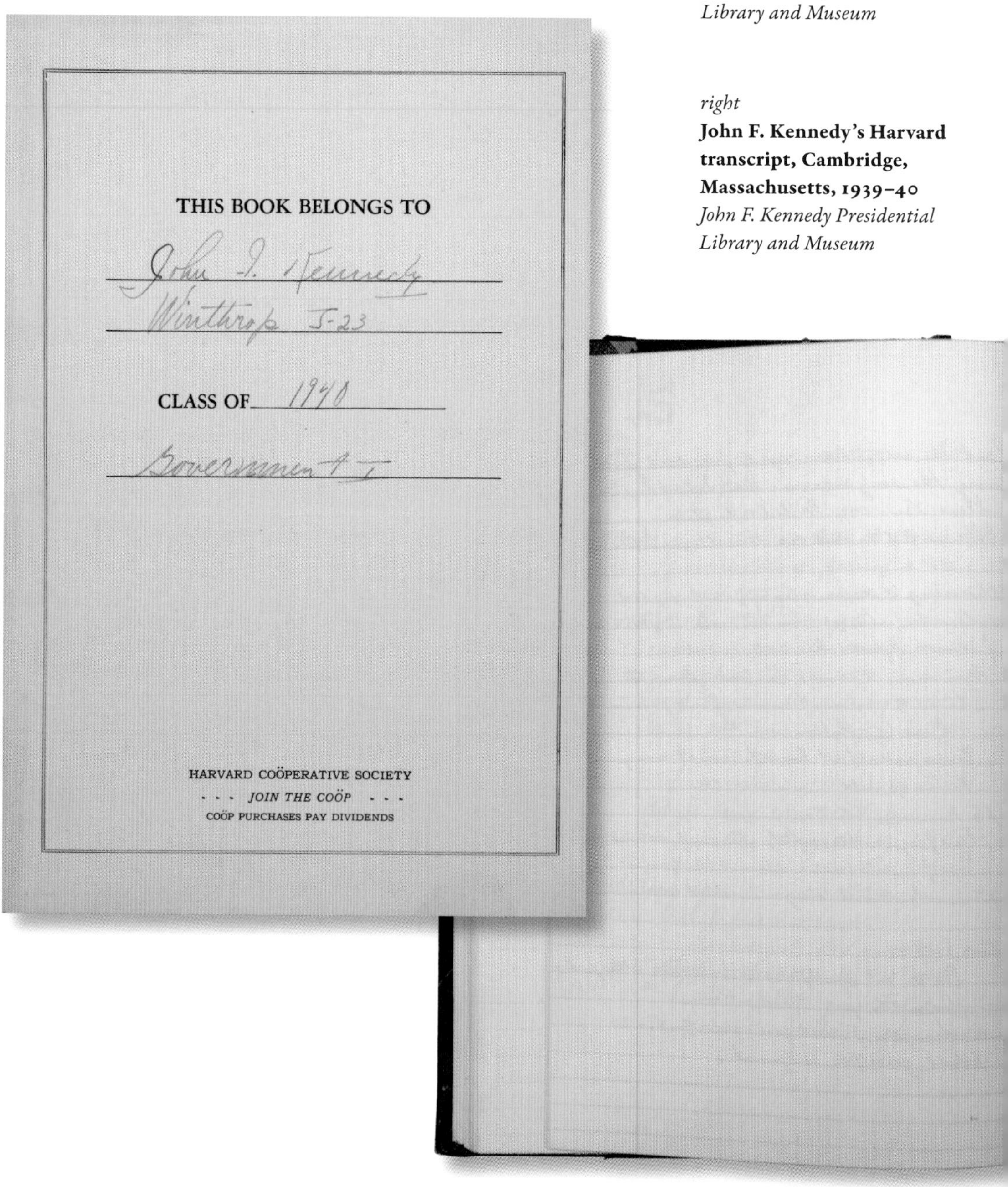

President John F. Kennedy's older brother, Joe, announced when he was a young boy that he would be the first Catholic to become President. On the other hand, John F. Kennedy seemed somewhat less ambitious. At Harvard University, he was active in student groups and sports. He worked hard in his history and government classes, but his grades remained only average.

In 1937, John F. Kennedy's father was appointed by President Franklin D. Roosevelt to be U.S. ambassador to Great Britain, and Kennedy became very interested in European politics and world affairs. After a summer visit to England and other countries in Europe, Kennedy returned to Harvard more eager to learn about history and government and to keep up with current events. When he was a senior at Harvard, he wrote his thesis on why Great Britain was unprepared for war with Germany. It was later published as a book called *Why England Slept*.

**Pages from John F.
Kennedy's manuscript
titled "Appeasement
of Munich" on which
was based his book *Why
England Slept*, 1940, title
page and preface**
*John F. Kennedy Presidential
Library and Museum*

*right*

**Lyndon B. Johnson's Southwest Texas Teacher's College transcript, side 1. San Marcos, Texas, 1930**

*Lyndon Baines Johnson Presidential Library and Museum*

*below*

**Lyndon B. Johnson's Teachers Permanent Certificate, 1930**

*Lyndon Baines Johnson Presidential Library and Museum*

Lyndon Johnson attended Southwest Texas Teacher's College (now Texas State University) but was forced to leave in order to save money. He obtained a teaching certificate and taught fifth, sixth, and seventh grades in the small town of Cotulla, Texas. He returned to college the following year and completed his bachelor of science degree in history and education. Johnson later said about his college years, "Here the seeds were planted from which grew my firm conviction that for the individual, education is the path to achievement and fulfillment; for the Nation, it is a path to a society that is not only free but civilized; and for the world, it is the path to peace—for it is education that places reason over force."

# College

As he had in high school, Richard Nixon continued to compete in oratorical contests. At Whittier College, he was a member of the Southern Conference Champion Debating Team in 1933 and was the Southern Conference Intercollegiate extemporaneous speaking champion in 1934. Richard Nixon graduated second in his class from Whittier College in 1934 with a major in history and government. He was president of his class in 1930 and vice president of the student body in 1933. He was awarded a scholarship to attend Duke University Law School.

WHAT CAN I BELIEVE

A series of essays prepared by Richard M. Nixon during his Senior year of study at Whittier College during the 1933-1934 school year in the course "Philosophy of Christian Reconstruction".

A

WHAT CAN I BELIEVE?

I. How Do I Work?                                    October 9, 1933

Self analysis must certainly be the most difficult and the most revealing study that a college student can undertake. Being a supposedly educated senior, I thought that it would be quite a simple matter to put my beliefs in writing. Upon looking further into the problem I found that far from being a logically minded college student, I was completely lost in attempting any close analysis of my ideas and methods. However, I shall place my ideas about certain philosophical problems before the reader and let him see what a jumbled mess can be made of a man's brain and ideas by a modern college education.

The first problem which comes up is the one of method. What method do I use, or better, what method does my intelligence tell me to use. In making a short study of English philosophers during the past year I became an intense admirer of David Hume. Hume's method, more than that of any other philosopher of whom I know was the most logical, the most scientific. Bacon had described the scientific method but had not used it. Hobbes and Locke had attempted to work without letting tradition and preconceived ideas interfere, but they too failed. Hume, however, took absolutely nothing for granted. He tested all systems of thought by experiment and reason. Therefore, in view of my limited knowledge of methods of thought, I must accept that one which appears most logical and reasonable to me. The scientific method is the one my experience tells me to use. Taking nothing for granted, arriving at conclusions through experiment, using these conclusions as the basis for an hypothesis, and then proving the hypothesis by more experiment! This is my method, the scientific method as near as I can describe it.

But immediately I find myself confronted with an unanswerable problem. Logic tells me to take nothing for granted, but what can I do with religion? My starting point should be something which conforms to the scientific ideal, not a God or a force whose reality is ascertained by intuition. The true scientist would have no arbitrary starting point. He would experiment and reason with the purpose of finding one. Years of training in the home and church have had their effect on my thinking however. My parents, "fundamental Quakers", had ground into me, with the aid of the church, all the fundamental ideas in their strictest interpretation. The infallibility and literal correctness of the bible, the miracles, even the whale story, all these I accepted as facts when I entered college four years ago. Even then I could not forget the admonition to not be misled by college professors who might be a little too liberal in their views! Many of those childhood ideas have been destroyed but there are some which I cannot bring myself to drop. To me, the greatness of the universe is too much for man to explain. I still believe that God is the creator, the first cause of all that exists. I still believe that He lives today, in some form, directing the destinies of the cosmos. How can I reconcile this idea with my scientific method? It is of course an unanswerable question. However, for the time being I shall accept the solution offered by Kant: that man can go only so far in his research and explanations; from that point on we must accept God. What is unknown to man, God knows. I shall use the scientific method to arrive at what concepts I can; then I shall call that great unknown world, God's world.

- 1 -

Now I am ready to chose an hypothesis with which to work. It is still my firm
f, due perhaps to my early training, that God created the universe as it is. There
been changes in the cosmos, in living creatures, etc., but I still believe that these
ges have been within the different "classes" themselves. For example, human beings
e created as they are, although their physical and mental beings have changed through
ages! I know that this idea is a laughing stock among competent scholars, but in view
y past education, or lack of education, I can maintain no other theory. Let me hasten
ay, however, that this view is not unsusceptible to further development. I am no
er a "seven day-er"! In declaring that God created the world, I am only acknow-
ing that my own mind is not capable of explaining it in any other way. How God
ted the world, I do not attempt to say; I am not able to understand that problem.
ieve, however, that I should make an attempt to understand as much about the world
possibly can. With this purpose in mind, I am going to attempt to prove the evolu-
y hypothesis. The concept of growth and improvement seems to fit into my scheme
ought exceedingly well. I am not able to say what evolutionary theory I intend to use.
t I do wish to do is to give a fair trial to all of them and to either accept or reject
n on their merits. Undoubtedly, of course, my concept of God as the creator will
erfere with my impartiality, but it is certain that I shall attempt to make that inter-
nce as small as possible. God then is my starting point, my great cause or what
will; I shall attempt to use the scientific method in proving an evolutionary hypo-
is as to the origin and development of the universe. Certainly, there could be no
e jumbled set of ideas than these. Let us hope that further study will unravel some
e crossed threads of my thought!

Finally I am confronted with what to me is the greatest problem of all. What
e purpose of all this study? Where am I heading for? Why not go ahead living and
et this problem of existence? We humans differ from the lower animals in that
re curious about such things. We are never satisfied with just living. We must
ugh know why we live. My purpose in making this study of philosophy is to get
earer picture of how I came to be on this earth, and to learn what my purpose in
is; I used to accept the biblical account of man's natural depravity and his pre-
ination on to heaven or to hell. My education has taught me that the bible, like all
r books, is a work of man and consequently has man made mistakes. Now I desire
nd a suitable explanation of man's and the universe's creation, an explanation that
fit not only with my idea of God but also with what my mind tells me is right. I
t to know why I am here in order that I may better find my place in life.

With this illogical method, starting point, hypothesis, and purpose, I am
ring into the field of philosophy. Where my study will lead I do not know, but
ainly any system of ideas would be better than this absurd collection of science,
gion and philosophy that I now have!

- 2 -

*left and above*
**Richard Nixon's "What
Can I Believe?" essay,
Whittier College, Whittier,
California, 1933**
*Richard Nixon Library and
Birthplace*

*right*
**Richard Nixon's Whittier
College grade report,
Whittier, California, 1934**
*Richard Nixon Library and
Birthplace*

WHITTIER COLLEGE
GRADE REPORT

STUDENT Nixon, Richard

CLASS Senior

REPORT FOR
SEMESTER ENDING June 9, 1934

SUBJECTS:

Hist. 202 A
Hist. 110 A
Phil. 138 A
Eng. 14 A
P.E. 82 W
P.E. 72 B
Glee Club A

A—EXCEPTIONAL
B—SUPERIOR
C—AVERAGE
D—POOR
COND.—CONDITIONED
F—FAILED
P—PASSED WITHOUT GRADE
W—WITHDRAWN

# College

From 1931 to 1935 Gerald Ford attended the University of Michigan at Ann Arbor, where he majored in economics and political science. He graduated with a bachelor of arts degree in June 1935. For Mother's Day, Ford sent his mother warm wishes saying his "financial condition" prevented him from sending flowers or candy. Although he received modest assistance from his family, Ford paid for his college education with part-time jobs and a small scholarship from his high school.

*above and right*
**Gerald R. Ford's letter to his mother, Dorothy Ford, wishing her a happy Mother's Day, May 12, 1933**
*Gerald R. Ford Presidential Library and Museum*

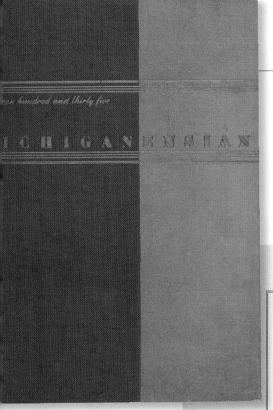

*above and right*

**Gerald R. Ford's University of Michigan yearbook,** *Michiganensian,* **Ann Arbor, Michigan, 1935**

*Gerald R. Ford Presidential Library and Museum*

**Harvey Smith** . . . because he spent two years at Illinois where he became the only Michigan man to beat Michigan out of a conference track championship; because he decided to come to Michigan and be a forester and incidentally to show the coaches what a superb track man he was; because the coaching staff persuaded him to come back for another year and be a "master forester" and because he admits to a very few of his close friends that he never would have had such ambitions if it hadn't been for the A.O.Pi president who later decided he spent too much time training for championships; because he's a Phi Gam and incidentally a Michigamua; and because he added an All Conference Medal to his lengthy string of victory charms.

**Jerry Ford** . . . because the football team chose him as their most valuable player; because he was a good student and got better grades than anyone else on the squad; because he put the D.K.E. house back on a paying basis; because he never smokes, drinks, swears, or tells dirty stories, qualities quite novel among the rest of his fraternity brothers; because he's exceedingly bashful but broke forth the middle of his senior year with a date; because he has decided to coach football at Yale and incidentally to study law; and because he's not a bit fraudulent and we can't find anything really nasty to say about him.

**Robert Ward** . . . because he's the most locquacious lubricator that we know of; because he was the big gun in the Senior State Street Party (hired airplanes, jackasses and the like) and then after taking a terrific beating persuaded the Washtenaw boys to let him take over their treasurer's job; because he pretends to be a woman hater but has an enviable appeal to the weaker sex; because he took all the available ad writing courses to qualify himself for the Daily job but had to be content with writing ads for Goldman's; because he's the originator of the famous Friday afternoon beer lecturers and can wield two full glasses with with the best of them.

# College

Jimmy Carter attended Georgia School of Technology during the summer of 1942 in order to fulfill the admission requirements for the U.S. Naval Academy. Jimmy Carter had dreamed of attending as a boy. In fact, when he was only seven years old, he wrote the Naval Academy requesting the entrance requirements.

*above left*
**Jimmy Carter's letter to his mother, Lillian Carter, from Georgia School of Technology, May 10, 1942**
*Jimmy Carter Presidential Library and Museum*

*above right*
**Jimmy Carter's letter to his mother, Lillian Carter, from United States Naval Academy, July 6, 1943**
*Jimmy Carter Presidential Library and Museum*

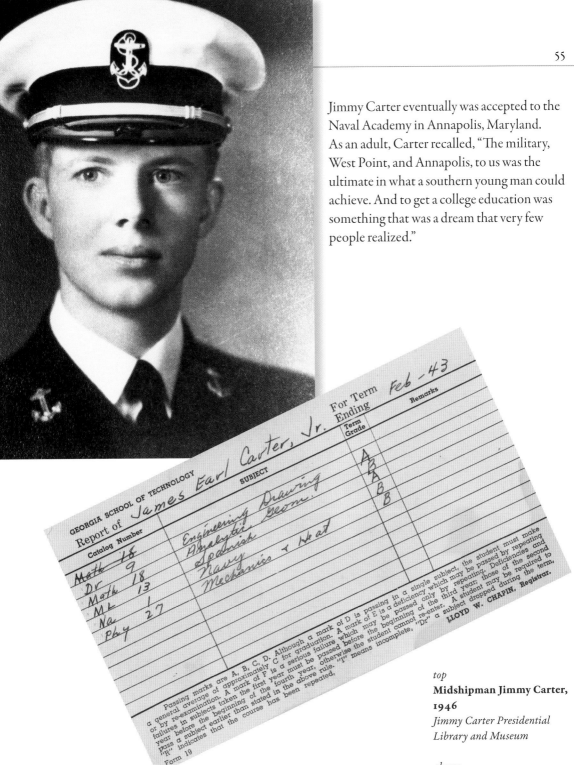

Jimmy Carter eventually was accepted to the Naval Academy in Annapolis, Maryland. As an adult, Carter recalled, "The military, West Point, and Annapolis, to us was the ultimate in what a southern young man could achieve. And to get a college education was something that was a dream that very few people realized."

GEORGIA SCHOOL OF TECHNOLOGY

Report of *James Earl Carter, Jr.*

For Term Ending Feb - 43

| Catalog Number | SUBJECT | Term Grade | Remarks |
|---|---|---|---|
| Math 18 | Engineering Drawing | A | |
| Dr 9 | Analytic Geom. | B | |
| Math 18 | Spanish | A | |
| ML 13 | Navy | B | |
| Phy 27 | Mechanics + Heat | B | |

Passing marks are A, B, C, D. Although a mark of D is passing in a single subject, the student must make a general average of approximately C for graduation. A mark of E is a deficiency which may be passed by repeating or by re-examination. A mark of F is a serious failure which may be passed only by repeating. Deficiencies and failures in subjects taken the first year must be passed before the beginning of the third year; those of the second year before the beginning of the fourth year, otherwise the student cannot re-enter. A student may be required to pass a subject earlier than stated in the above rule. "Dr" a subject dropped during the term, "I" means incomplete, "R" indicates that the course has been repeated.

LLOYD W. CHAPIN, Registrar.

Form 19

*top*
**Midshipman Jimmy Carter, 1946**
*Jimmy Carter Presidential Library and Museum*

*above*
**Jimmy Carter's Georgia School of Technology report card, Atlanta, Georgia, 1943**
*Jimmy Carter Presidential Library and Museum*

## College

George H.W. Bush graduated from Phillips Academy, Andover, Massachusetts, on his 18th birthday, June 12, 1942, with World War II raging on two fronts. That same day, although he had been accepted at Yale University, he enlisted in the U.S. Navy as a seaman second class. He received his wings and commission in June 1943 and was the youngest pilot in the U.S. Navy at that time.

*above*
**George H.W. Bush, U.S. Navy Primary Flight Training, Minnesota, ca. 1942**
*George H.W. Bush Presidential Library and Museum*

*right*
**U.S. Navy pilot George H.W. Bush in the cockpit of an Avenger, ca. 1942**
*George H.W. Bush Presidential Library and Museum*

**Phi Beta Kappa**

Founded December 5, 1776

This Writing Certifies That

George Herbert Walker Bush

Was made a member of ΦBK by action of the

Alpha of Connecticut at Yale University

in recognition of high attainments in liberal scholarship

In Witness Whereof, the President and the Secretary
of the Chapter have hereunto affixed their signatures

May 15, 1948

When George H.W. Bush left the Navy after World War II, he entered Yale University, where he pursued a degree in economics. He graduated Phi Beta Kappa in 1948. On January 6, 1945, George H.W. Bush married Barbara Pierce of Rye, New York. Their first son, the future President George W. Bush, was born while his father was a student at Yale.

*above*
**George H.W. Bush's Certificate of Membership to Phi Beta Kappa, Yale University, New Haven, Connecticut, May 15, 1948**
*George H.W. Bush Presidential Library and Museum*

*right*
**George H.W. and George W. Bush in matching Yale jerseys, ca. late 1946**
*George H.W. Bush Presidential Library and Museum*

# Men of Many Talents

*"And I don't think I would have become President if it hadn't been for school music."*

*William J. Clinton*

his is to ce
*Bill*
of the

into the
of the
**BAPT**

of the
*Clay*

As students, the modern Presidents developed their talents and learned new skills not only inside the classroom but also through enrichment and extracurricular activities. Some of these young men played musical instruments and sang. Others were debaters who competed in regional debate finals or were actors who wrote home excitedly about their first part in a play. The programs, sheet music, and award certificates preserved in the Presidential Libraries show the importance of these activities in the young men's lives. These documents, artifacts, and photographs show the wide interests and varied activities that both revealed and shaped the characters of the future Presidents.

*below right*
**Gerald R. Ford (third from left), age 23, and fellow rangers at the Canyon Station post in Yellowstone National Park, 1936**
*Gerald R. Ford Presidential Library and Museum*

*below*
**Baptist Training Union certificate, 1958**
*William J. Clinton Presidential Library and Museum*

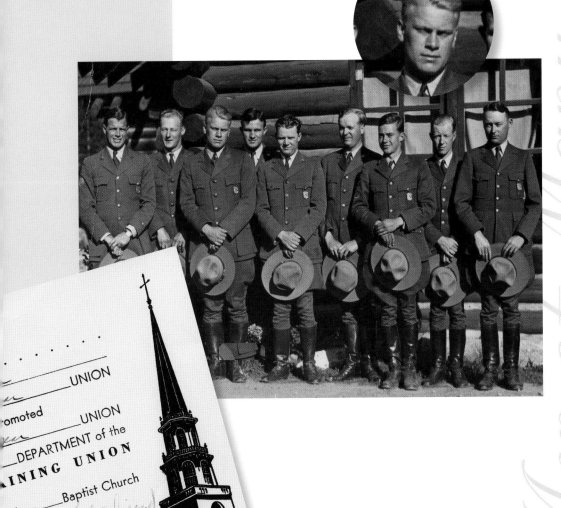

Men of Many Talents

In 1894, between his junior and senior years at Stanford University, Herbert Hoover worked for the U.S. Geological Survey, helping to map the geology near Lake Tahoe. Hoover is listed as the assistant in these geological maps covering Pyramid Peak, California.

*left*
**Geological Atlas of the United States, 1896**
*National Archives, Records of the United States Geological Survey*

In addition to serving as Secretary of the Glee Club, Franklin Roosevelt was also editor-in-chief of the *Harvard Crimson*, the undergraduate newspaper, a member of the Harvard Republican Club, and librarian for the Hasty Pudding Club.

*left*
**Franklin D. Roosevelt in *The Wedding March*, as Uncle Bopaddy (far right), 1900**
*Franklin D. Roosevelt Presidential Library and Museum*

*top*
**Harvard Glee Club, Roosevelt is third from the left, bottom row, 1901**
*Franklin D. Roosevelt Presidential Library and Museum*

*right*
**Harvard freshman Glee Club poster, 1901**
*Franklin D. Roosevelt Presidential Library and Museum*

THE MEMBERS OF THE

HARVARD FRESHMAN

GLEE CLUB

WILL MEET TO-NIGHT AT 7.30 O'CLOCK.

*President.*
*Secretary.*
*Leader.*

1904

Excited about acquiring his role at the last minute in the school play, *The Wedding March*, Franklin wrote immediately to give his parents the news.

*left*
**Franklin D. Roosevelt's letter home to parents while at Groton, February 11, 1900**
*Franklin D. Roosevelt Presidential Library and Museum*

28-283

GROTON SCHOOL,
GROTON, MASS.

Sunday.
Feb. 21ᵉ

My darling Mama and Papa,
Joyful news! I have a part in the play at last and entirely by accident. Jimmy Jackson had the part of the old hayseed countrified uncle of the bride. He is sick in Boston with rheumatic fever & water on the knee so wont be back again this term. I suppose it is criminal to rejoice but I cant help it! I've got his part, and it's one of the best in the play!!!! I have begun to learn it hard and shall have to work hard as the play is only ten days off. We have had 3 rehearsals last week & I did well I think, tho' I dont know my part yet. Remember, dont breathe a word to anyone yet, till the play-bills are out, & I will try to send you one this week.

All your letters of the

Harry Truman began taking piano lessons when he was about 12 years old, and he probably continued taking them for several years, until he had to go to work to help support his struggling family. He was a serious student and liked serious music. He could play some of his favorite Mozart and Chopin pieces all his life.

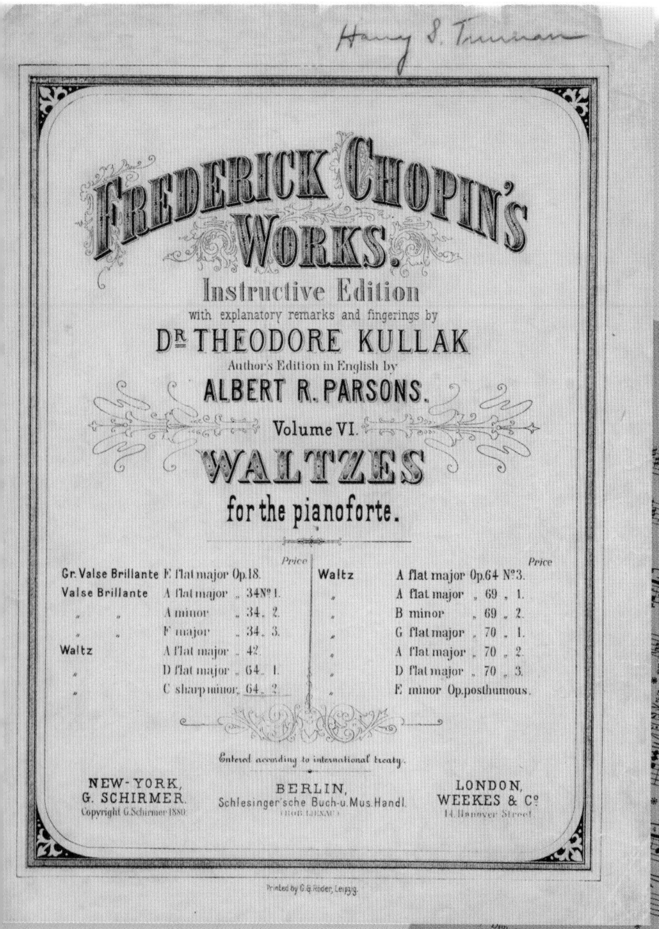

*above and right*
**Frederick Chopin's Works,**
© 1880
*Harry S. Truman Presidential Library and Museum*

The High School Department
OF THE
Johnson City Public School
ASSISTED BY MRS. S. E. JOHNSON
PRESENTS THE PLAY
"An Old Fashioned Mother"
THURSDAY NIGHT, MAY 3RD, 1923.

CAST OF CHARACTERS.

Deborah Underhill .................. A Mother in Israel
Annie Rae Ottmers.
Widder Bill Pindle ................. Leader of the Choir
Georgia Cammack.
Miss Lowizy Loviny Custard .... Plain Sewing and Gossip
Louise Casparis.
Isabel Simpscott ..................... The Village Belle
Kittie Clyde Ross.
Gloriana Perkins ..................... As Good as Gold
Margaret Johnson.
Sukey Pindle
John Underhill ...................... The Prodigal Son
Lyndon Johnson.
Charley Underhill ..................... The Elder Brother
Garland Galloway.
Brother Jonah Quackenbush ...... A Whited Sepulchre
John Dollahite.
Jeremiah Gosling, "Jerry" .............. A Merry Heart
Truman Fawcett.
Enoch Rose .............. An Outcast and a Wanderer
Cecil Redford.
Quintus Todd ..................... The County Sheriff
Charley Hunnicutt
The Village Choir.

Time: Twenty years ago. Place: The vil
ton in Northern New York.

SYNOPSIS.

ACT I—Settin' Room at the Underhill Fa
afternoon in late March. The Good Samarit

ACT II—Same scene, three years later.
noon. A Mother's Love.

ACT III—Same scene, two years late
autumn. The Prodigal Son.

ADMISSION, 15C AND 25C

Lyndon Johnson played John Underhill, the prodigal son, in the Johnson City High School senior play. An unenthusiastic student, Johnson nonetheless enjoyed such extracurricular activities as the debating club.

*left*
**Program from *An Old Fashioned Mother*, 1923**
*Lyndon Baines Johnson Presidential Library and Museum*

Richard Nixon enjoyed acting and was known in college for his character roles. He later met Pat, his future wife, when they were both cast in *The Dark Tower*.

PHILIP_____ RICHARD HARRIS
CYNTHIA_____ RUTH JOHNS
MRS RANDOLPH_____ LEONA OTT
EDNA_____ NORMA ALLEN
MRS OLIVER MARY ELEANOR HOLLOWELL
MR. ELDRIDGE_____ RICHARD NIXON

*above*
**Program from *Philip Goes Forth*, 1933–34 season**
*Courtesy of the Richard Nixon Library and Birthplace*

## Men of Many Talents

Gerald Ford is the only President to have earned the rank of Eagle Scout in the Boy Scouts. These Boy Scout award cards show the merit badges he earned, including for first aid, forestry, and animal husbandry.

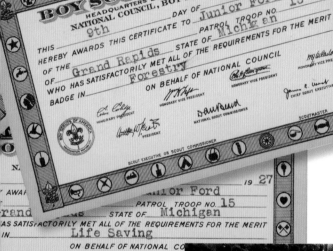

*left*
**Boy Scout Award cards, 1925–27, Grand Rapids, Michigan**
*Gerald R. Ford Presidential Library and Museum*

*right*
**Gerald R. Ford (first on left), age 16, with the Eagle Scout Guard of Honor at Mackinac Island State Park, Michigan, August 1929**
*Gerald R. Ford Presidential Library and Museum*

THIS IS TO CERTIFY THAT

Gerald Ford

IS A MEMBER OF

## Delta Kappa Epsilon Fraternity,

HAVING BEEN DULY AND REGULARLY ELECTED THERETO
AND INITIATED THEREIN BY_____Omicron_____
CHAPTER OF DELTA KAPPA EPSILON ON THE____7th____
DAY OF__May__, __1932__
IN WITNESS WHEREOF THE COUNCIL OF DELTA KAPPA
EPSILON HAS HEREUNTO CAUSED THIS CERTIFICATE TO BE
SIGNED AND SEALED BY ITS PRESIDENT AND SECRETARY THIS
__20th__ DAY OF__May__, __1932__

(SEAL)                    President of Delta Kappa Epsilon.

ATTEST:

Secretary of the Council of Delta Kappa Epsilon.

"TRANSLATION"

*left*
**Delta Kappa Epsilon
certificate, May 2, 1932**
*Gerald R. Ford Presidential
Library and Museum*

*below*
**High school advertisement,
souvenir program of the
Union High School vs.
South High School football
game, November 27, 1930**
*Gerald R. Ford Presidential
Library and Museum*

At the University of Michigan, Gerald Ford
joined the Delta Kappa Epsilon fraternity.
Unable to pay for room and board, Ford lived
at the fraternity house, where he worked as a
dishwasher to pay his rent. As captain of his
high school football team, Gerald Ford was
asked to model in this advertisement.

UNION — vs. — SOUTH

THANKSGIVING
DAY

The popular Captains of
these two Football Teams
—wearing—

UNIVERSITY
STYLES
*by*
LEARBURY

GERALD FORD                    TED BURGESS

*Ted Burgess, Captain of Union High, is a member of
The Varsity Club, his third year playing on the team and
first year as Captain . . . . Gerald Ford is a member of
The Varsity Club, Latin Club, and Track Team and first
year as Captain of South High.*

These models, together with other styles of suits
and overcoats, tailored and styled by "Learbury,"
may be seen at our store. These garments are styled
to meet the demands of the young men and are
always correct.

MAY WE SHOW YOU?

HOUSEMAN & JONES
*79 Years a Grand Rapids Institution*

George and Barbara Bush met at a country club dance in Connecticut during Christmas break in 1941. She was a 16-year-old student at a Charleston, South Carolina, prep school. He was a senior at Phillips Academy in Andover, Massachusetts. When they returned to their schools, they kept in touch by writing letters. In a letter from 1942, Barbara accepted Poppy's (his nickname) invitation to the Phillips Academy Promenade.

*below*
**Letter from Barbara Pierce (Bush) to Poppy (George H.W. Bush), Charleston, South Carolina, 1942**
*George H.W. Bush Presidential Library and Museum*

*left*

**George H.W. Bush at summer camp, 1939**

*George H.W. Bush Presidential Library and Museum*

*below*

**George H.W. Bush (immediate left of clock) with the Skull and Bones, Yale University, New Haven, Connecticut, ca. 1947**

*George H.W. Bush Presidential Library and Museum*

## Men of Many Talents

At Hot Springs High School, the music teacher and band director, Virgil Spurlin, selected Bill Clinton to be the band major. In addition to playing in the school marching band, Bill played the saxophone in the Stardusters, the school's dance band.

*left*
**Music Stand, Stardusters Jazz Band from Hot Springs High School, ca. 1964**
*William J. Clinton Presidential Library and Museum*

*left*
**Bill Clinton holding his saxophone at home, Hot Springs, Arkansas, August 19, 1958**
*William J. Clinton Presidential Library and Museum*

**United States Senate**
COMMITTEE ON FOREIGN RELATIONS

July 25, 1963

Mr. and Mrs. Roger M. Clinton
213 Scully Street
Hot Springs, Arkansas

Dear Mr. and Mrs. Clinton:

Last Monday, Senator McClellan and I had
lunch with your son and Larry Taunton when they
were here for Boys' Nation.

It was a privilege to be with these boys.
Your son is a fine young man, and I am sure you are
proud of him. I just want you to know that it was
a pleasure to have met him.

With all good wishes, I am

Sincerely yours,

J. W. Fulbright

JWF:kj

While he was still in high school, Bill met Senator J. William Fulbright, a Democratic senator from Arkansas, at Boys Nation. Clinton admired Senator Fulbright and later, while a student at Georgetown University, worked part-time for the Senate Foreign Relations Committee, which was headed by Fulbright. The senator was influential in guiding Clinton in his early political career.

*above*
**Letter from Senator Fulbright to Bill Clinton's parents, July 25, 1963**
*William J. Clinton Presidential Library and Museum*

*left*
**Hot Springs High School seniors who were National Merit semifinalists, Bill Clinton (second from right), with Bobby Haness, Pat Brady, Jim McDougal, and Sammy White, Hot Springs, Arkansas, 1963**
*William J. Clinton Presidential Library and Museum*

**Ronald Reagan (front row at left, hand on chin) sitting with other caddies for the Lincoln Highway Ladies Golf Tournament, 1922**
*Ronald Reagan Presidential Library and Museum*

# A Winning Spirit

"*Politics is an astonishing profession — it has ... enabled me to go from being an obscure member of the junior varsity at Harvard to being an honorary member of the Football Hall of Fame.*"

*John F. Kennedy*

*below*
**Harvard second football team, John F. Kennedy is standing in the second row from the back, third from right, 1937**
*John F. Kennedy Presidential Library and Museum*

*below*
**Jimmy Carter (No. 10) with the Plains High School basketball team, ca. 1939**
*Jimmy Carter Presidential Library and Museum*

*bottom*
**Dixon High School football team (Ronald Reagan is fourth from the left, in the first row), 1925**
*Ronald Reagan Presidential Library and Museum*

Most of the 20th-century Presidents participated enthusiastically in sports throughout their time in school; some of them even got into college based partially upon their sports talents. Most of these future leaders continued their sports interests and participation even when they became President. Whether it was football, baseball, basketball, golf, or the swim team, the dynamics of sports were an important part of each young man's formative years. A few were gifted athletes, but all of them learned sportsmanship and teamwork through athletics.

Winning Spirit

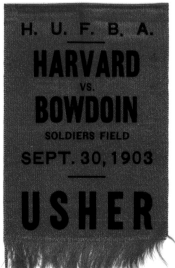

## A Winning Spirit

Although not a star athlete himself, Franklin Roosevelt enjoyed participating in and viewing athletic competitions at Harvard. At Harvard football, baseball, and track competitions, Roosevelt would wear a badge in support of his school.

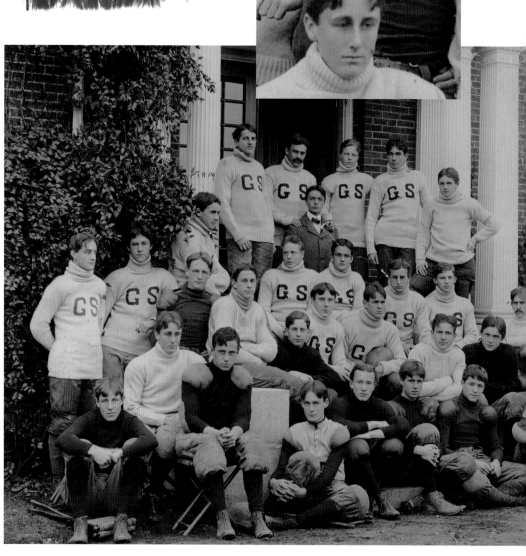

Franklin Roosevelt's first opportunity to participate in team sports was at Groton. In his senior year, he was manager of the baseball team, which, to him, was an important but "thankless task."

*below*
**Franklin D. Roosevelt playing golf at Campobello (while away from school), 1904**
*Franklin D. Roosevelt Presidential Library and Museum*

*top left*
**Harvard University badge, Bowdoin vs. Harvard, September 30, 1903**
*Franklin D. Roosevelt Presidential Library and Museum*

*above*
**Baseball team at Groton (Franklin D. Roosevelt is third from right in the back row), 1899**
*Franklin D. Roosevelt Presidential Library and Museum*

*left*
**Football team at Groton (Franklin D. Roosevelt is second from left, first row), 1899**
*Franklin D. Roosevelt Presidential Library and Museum*

## Athletics

### By Dwight Eisenhower

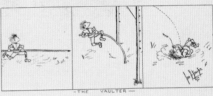

E ARLY in the fall of 1908, the High School boys organized an Athletic Association for the year. After electing Dwight Eisenhower president, Harry Makins vice-president and Herbert Sommers secretary and treasurer, we proceeded to do business.

Deciding not to play any base ball in the fall, we started on football at once. Bruce Hurd was elected captain, and soon a large number of candidates for the squad were out working. After two weeks of hard work, Captain Hurd decided on the following team:

Left end.........................Huffman
Left tackle.......................Ingersoll
Left guard........................Pattin
Center...........................Funk
Right guard......................Weckle
Right tackle.....................Hurd
Right end.................D. Eisenhower
Quarter..........................Merrifield
Left half........................Makins
Right half.......................Sommers
Full back.................E. Eisenhower

We were deprived of our coach, but nevertheless, turned out a very creditable team. Unfortunately, however, only four games were played during the season, not giving the team a chance to prove its ability. But for the games that were played, the students supported the team loyally, and time and again the boys surmounted great difficulties, cheered on by the fierce enthusiasm displayed by our rooters.

After the football season closed, we had to spend the winter dreaming of past victories and future glories, for A. H. S. boasts of no indoor gymnasium, and basket ball was never played here. But we improved the condition of the Association, by drawing up a constitution, which makes the organization a permanent one, and each year it will be simply a question of electing new officers.

Thanking the citizens of the town who have taken such an interest in the High School Athletics, and also our fellow classmates for their loyalty to us, we are yours for future victories on the gridiron by teams of dear old A. H. S.

**FOOTBALL SCHEDULE**

Abilene vs. Junction City at Junction City.
Abilene vs. Junction City at Abilene.
Abilene vs. Chapman at Abilene.
Abilene vs. Agricultural College at Abilene.

— THE VAULTER —

Dwight Eisenhower played football and baseball in high school. In 1908 he helped form and was elected president of the Athletic Association, which was responsible for raising funds for the football and baseball teams.

*top*
**Helianthus, Abilene High
School yearbook, 1909**
*Dwight D. Eisenhower Presidential
Library and Museum*

*left*
**Dwight D. Eisenhower kicking
football at West Point, 1912**
*Dwight D. Eisenhower Presidential
Library and Museum*

*above*

**Abilene High School football
team (Dwight D. Eisenhower
is in the back row, third from
left), 1909**

*Dwight D. Eisenhower
Presidential Library and Museum*

## A Winning Spirit

Ford was all-city and all-state center in his high school senior year. He later recalled his coach teaching "You play to win . . . but you always play within the rules."

*left*
**Gerald R. Ford's letter sweater from the University of Michigan**
*Gerald R. Ford Presidential Library and Museum*

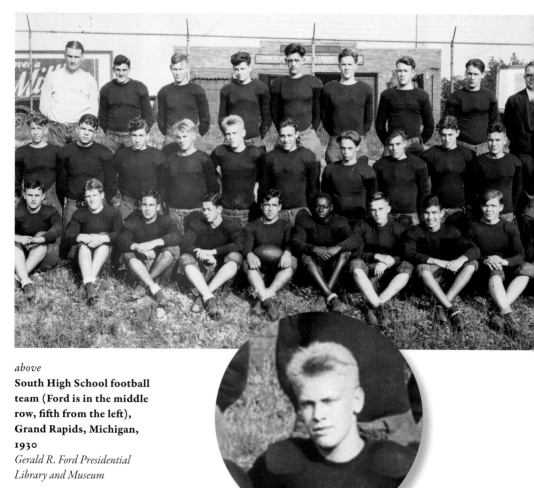

*above*
**South High School football team (Ford is in the middle row, fifth from the left), Grand Rapids, Michigan, 1930**
*Gerald R. Ford Presidential Library and Museum*

GREEN BAY FOOTBALL CORPORATION
"PACKERS"
GREEN BAY, WISCONSIN

Feb. 11, 1935

Gerald Ford of Michigan
University, Michigan
Ann Arbor,

Dear Ford:

While on the Coast you told me you were un-
decided in regard to playing professional football.

We plan on signing a center for the coming
season and will pay you $110.00 per game if you wish to join
the "Packers". Our league schedule is not drafted but we usually
play fourteen games. We pay in full after each contest and all
players are paid whether they play or not and naturally, all
injured players are paid immediately after each game.

Will appreciate an early reply.

With kindest personal regards, I am

Sincerely,

GREEN BAY FOOTBALL CORPORATION

ELL*GC

*left*

**Letter from the Green
Bay Football Corporation
to Gerald R. Ford,
February 11, 1935**
*Gerald R. Ford Presidential
Library and Museum*

*below*

**Gerald R. Ford on the field
at Michigan Stadium at the
University of Michigan,
Ann Arbor, Michigan, 1933**
*Gerald R. Ford Presidential
Library and Museum*

*below*

**Newspaper Clipping,
"All City Selections," 1930**
*Gerald R. Ford Presidential
Library and Museum*

A gifted center, Gerald Ford received offers to play
football from two professional football teams, the
Green Bay Packers and the Detroit Lions, after
graduation from the University of Michigan. He chose
instead to take a position as boxing coach and assistant
varsity football coach at Yale, where he hoped to attend
law school. He was admitted to the Law School in the
spring of 1938.

While attending high school at Phillips Academy—known also as Andover after the Massachusetts town where the school is located—George H.W. Bush was captain and first baseman of the baseball team. A gifted athlete, he also played basketball and soccer. As captain of the soccer team, George Bush received a letter of congratulations from his school's headmaster. Bush also played soccer at Yale and was on the co-national championship team in 1945.

**left**
**Letter to parents of George H.W. Bush from Phillips Academy headmaster, Claude M. Fuess, regarding the soccer team, November 18, 1941**
*George H.W. Bush Presidential Library and Museum*

**below**
**Student ticket to all athletic contests at Andover, 1941–42**
*George H.W. Bush Presidential Library and Museum*

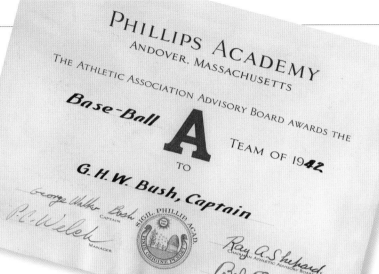

PHILLIPS ACADEMY
ANDOVER, MASSACHUSETTS

THE ATHLETIC ASSOCIATION ADVISORY BOARD AWARDS THE

Base-Ball **A** TEAM OF 19**42**

TO

G. H. W. Bush, Captain

George Walker Bush CAPTAIN
P. C. Welch MANAGER
SIGIL. PHILLIP ACAD.
Ray A. Shepard CHAIRMAN ATHLETIC ADVISORY BOARD
Bob Flather SECRETARY ATHLETIC ADVISORY BOARD

*above*
**Certificate for Andover
Letter in baseball, 1942**
*George H.W. Bush Presidential
Library and Museum*

*right*
**George H.W. Bush plays
baseball at Phillips
Academy, Andover,
Massachusetts, ca. 1942**
*George H.W. Bush Presidential
Library and Museum*

# A Winning Spirit

*left*
**Lyndon B. Johnson playing baseball, as catcher, 1923**
*Lyndon Baines Johnson Presidential Library and Museum*

*below*
**Ronald Reagan, on Eureka College swim team, ca. 1928**
*Ronald Reagan Presidential Library and Museum*

*above*
**Harvard swim team (John F. Kennedy is in the back row, third from the left), ca. 1936–37**
*John F. Kennedy Presidential Library and Museum*

*right*
**George H.W. Bush (first on the left, in the first row), Yale Baseball team, 1946**
*George H.W. Bush Presidential Library and Museum*

Bush was also a talented first baseman. While he was on the baseball team at Yale, his team went to the first two College World Series in 1947 and 1948.

# Memories

*"Iowa, in those years as in these, was filled with days of school—and who does not remember with a glow some gentle woman who with infinite patience and kindness drilled into us those foundations we know today."*

*Herbert Hoover*

"HERBERT HOOVER
The Boy, The Man, The President."

I was Herbert Hoover's Teacher in 1884 and 1885; he was ten years old at that time, was in the Third Grade, advanced to the Fourth during the School year. He was studious and tractable; he had a wonderful Mother, and she it was who laid the foundation in the first ten years of his life that, with his education and self efficiency, made him the great man he is today. I feel the honor that I, as his teacher, may have had a part in tuiding his boy-hood; all these things working with God's plan to raise up a man to tuide our Nation aright at this critical time.

Herbert was a real boy, loved play, but his lessons came first. I think I never needed to make him do work over, nor did I ever punish him for not having lessons; my school was a bunch of live-wires and something had to be done to entertain them aside from dull Spelling, Arithmetic, and Geography, so every day at a certain period I told them some of the wonders of the world---oil wells were new them, Glaciers were used, which thrilled the boys, especially Herbert.

His home wassbroken up by the death of his Mother in February, 1885; his Father died in 1880. He lived with his Great Uncle Allan Hoover until August of that year; and his Mother's brother John Minthorn invited him to come to Salem, Oregon, and have a home with his children and be one of his household, and he travelled to the then Far West.

Before he left Iowa, these pupils, thirty-seven of them, decided to visit their School Teacher, and one of them borrowed a team of old mules and a hay wagon and came to my new home in the country to spend the day and have dinner. They came and we all enjoyed the visit, had a dinner that gave unalloyed joy to boys and girls of ten years. That is my last contact with Herbert Hoover as a boy.

He graduated from High School, and his Uncle John said, "Now, Herbert, I have put you through High School; you take one year and go to work; if you make good I will help you through the University." Leland Stanford was just now struggling to life and every one was anxious for a University in the West. John Minthorn was a good man, stern and of strong character, in the real estate business. Herbert went to work in his office; and it was said he was as good as an encyclopedia--if any one wanted to know anything in the business the answer was "Ask Herbert, he knows," and he knew. At the end of the year he had made good, had money in his pocket, but not so with hisgood Uncle; he had failed, had nothing, and Herbert said "W hat shall I do, I have no money and few friends? I know what I will do--I know a man who will put me through Leland Stanford; that is Herbert Hoover." And he did it. He graduated in 1895, just ten years from the time he went to school to me he was a graduate mining engineer by his own efforts.

He went to the gold mines up in Grass Valley and Nevada City, California, with his diploma. I have visited this beautiful mountain sppt. But Herbert found a diploma does not draw a salary, and so he donned his work clothes and went down into the mines. When some one met him pushing a wheel barrow and said,

Mollie Carran was Herbert Hoover's grade school teacher. In his memoirs, Hoover, who was orphaned at age 9, recalled, "[Mollie] strove to secure me for adoption. But Mollie was then unmarried, and the others insisted that family experience was a first necessity."

*left*
**Mollie Carran article, "Herbert Hoover: The Boy, The Man, The President," 1957, page 1**
*Herbert Hoover Presidential Library and Museum*

Long after their schooldays were over, these 20th-century Presidents
often reflected on their school experiences and the value of
education. Memoirs, scrapbooks, and letters reveal the wide range of
educational influences that shaped their lives. Many of the Presidents
were guided by and fondly recalled a special teacher. Whatever their
station in life at the time, wherever in America they were educated,
and whatever circumstances they faced, each young man developed a
special regard for schooling and the importance of education. These
Presidential souvenirs, saved by the Libraries, illustrate what these
leaders accomplished, remembered, and valued in the classrooms of
their youth.

Groton Headmaster Endicott Peabody
maintained a lifelong friendship with Franklin D.
Roosevelt. Not only did he send birthday cards to
Franklin every year, Peabody performed the
ceremony when FDR and Eleanor married.
Peabody attended Roosevelt's inauguration in
1933 and prayed with FDR before the ceremony.

*above and right*
**Reader's Digest** article,
**"Thank you Miss Gray,"**
**1959, pages 1 and 2**
*Herbert Hoover Presidential
Library and Museum*

When asked to write about the best advice he had ever received, Herbert Hoover wrote about Miss Jennie Gray. Miss Gray was not one of Herbert's teachers, but through her he learned the value of books beyond textbooks. His Quaker upbringing did not permit much reading beyond the Bible or the encyclopedia, and Miss Gray introduced him to books such as *Ivanhoe* and *David Copperfield*.

Rebelling against the structured life at Choate, John F. Kennedy and several of his friends formed the "Muckers," a term that the headmaster used for boys that did not live up to Choate's standards.

*above*
**John F. Kennedy and fellow "Muckers," ca. 1934**
*John F. Kennedy Presidential Library and Museum*

*left*
**John F. Kennedy's Choate scrapbook, Bronxville, New York, 1933–35**
*John F. Kennedy Presidential Library and Museum*

# *Memories*

In his inaugural address, Jimmy Carter drew attention to the influence of one of his teachers by quoting her early in the speech, "As my high school teacher, Miss Julia Coleman, used to say: 'We must adjust to changing times and still hold to unchanging principles.'"

Miss Coleman shaped Jimmy's life. She encouraged him to join the debate team in order to overcome his shyness and learn to articulate his position on issues.

*below*

**Jimmy Carter's inaugural address, January 20, 1977, page 1**

*Jimmy Carter Presidential Library and Museum*

INAUGURAL SPEECH
FOURTH DRAFT

*Cor –*
*This is your draft with*
*only suggested additions as marked.*
*Thought you might need it to ~~make~~ to do*
*your own final editing.*
*Jil*

*Final draft*
*JC*

FOR MYSELF AND OUR NATION, I WANT TO THANK MY PREDECESSOR
FOR ALL HE HAS DONE TO HEAL OUR LAND.

*IN THIS*
~~IN THE RITUAL WE OBSERVE TODAY, ONCE AGAIN WITH AN~~ OUTWARD
AND PHYSICAL CEREMONY WE ATTEST *once again* TO THE INNER AND SPIRITUAL STRENGTH
OF OUR NATION. [~~AS ALWAYS, THIS PASSAGE MARKS THE CONTINUITY OF~~
~~PAST PROMISES AND THE HOPE FOR NEW BEGINNINGS.~~]

HERE BEFORE ME IS THE BIBLE USED IN THE INAUGURATION OF OUR
FIRST PRESIDENT IN 1789, AND I HAVE JUST TAKEN MY OWN OATH OF
OFFICE ON THE BIBLE MY MOTHER GAVE ME *a few* ~~MANY~~ YEARS AGO, OPENED TO
A TIMELESS ADMONITION FROM THE ANCIENT PROPHET MICAH:

"HE HATH SHOWED THEE, O MAN, WHAT IS GOOD; AND WHAT DOTH
THE LORD REQUIRE OF THEE, BUT TO DO JUSTLY, AND TO LOVE MERCY,
AND TO WALK HUMBLY WITH THY GOD." (MICAH 6:8)

*As my high school teacher, Miss Julia Coleman,*
*used to say, "We must adjust to changing times*
*and still hold to unchanging principles."*

*left*
**Julia Coleman, Jimmy Carter's high school teacher, ca. 1930**
*Jimmy Carter Presidential Library and Museum*

*below*
**Julia Coleman and Young Thomas Sheffield, teachers at Plains High School, ca. 1930s**
*Jimmy Carter Presidential Library and Museum*

# Graduation

*"Education is the cornerstone of our Freedom."*

*Lyndon B. Johnson*

For each future President, graduation represented not only an end to his studies but also a new beginning as each pursued another level of school or began his professional life. This passage also signified the beginning of young adulthood and brought each of them farther along the path to public service and closer to the White House.

*left*
**Dwight D. Eisenhower's Abilene High School diploma, Abilene, Kansas, 1909**
*Dwight D. Eisenhower Presidential Library and Museum*

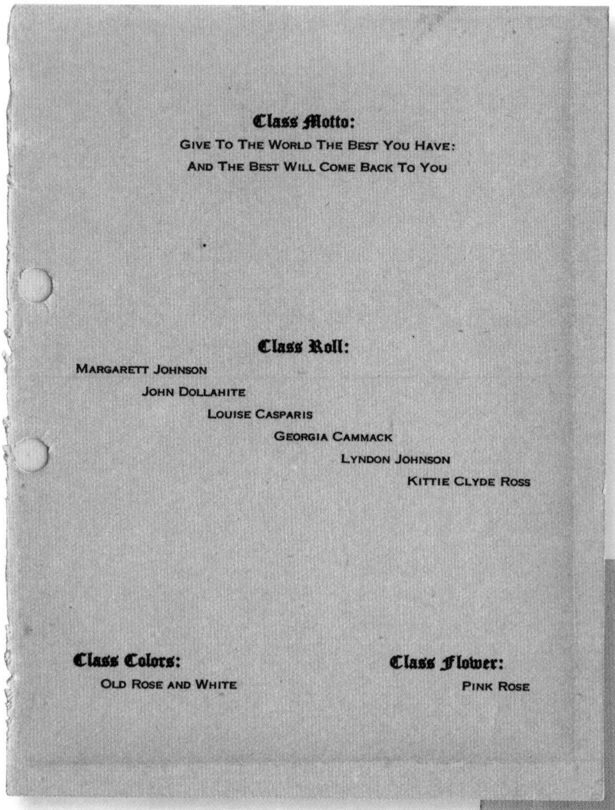

**Class Motto:**
GIVE TO THE WORLD THE BEST YOU HAVE:
AND THE BEST WILL COME BACK TO YOU

**Class Roll:**
MARGARETT JOHNSON
JOHN DOLLAHITE
LOUISE CASPARIS
GEORGIA CAMMACK
LYNDON JOHNSON
KITTIE CLYDE ROSS

**Class Colors:**
OLD ROSE AND WHITE

**Class Flower:**
PINK ROSE

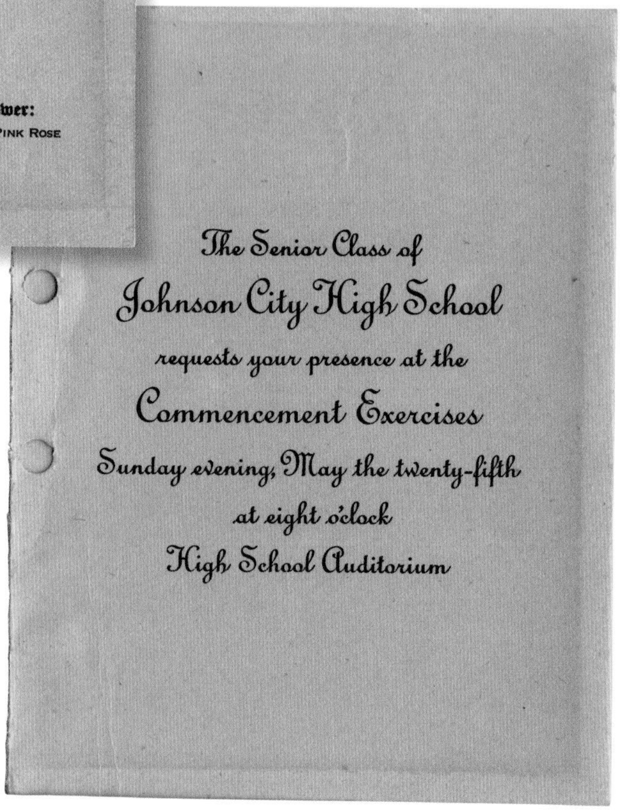

*above and right*
**Lyndon B. Johnson's
high school graduation
invitation, 1924**
*Lyndon Baines Johnson
Presidential Library
and Museum*

The Senior Class of
*Johnson City High School*
requests your presence at the
**Commencement Exercises**
Sunday evening, May the twenty-fifth
at eight o'clock
High School Auditorium

*top left*
**Portrait of Lyndon
B. Johnson, Southwest
Texas Teacher's College,
San Marcos, Texas, ca.
1927**
*Lyndon Baines Johnson
Presidential Library
and Museum*

*top right*
**Bill Clinton,
1964**
*Courtesy of William
J. Clinton*

*right*
**John F. Kennedy, Harvard
University, class of 1940,
June 20, 1940**
*John F. Kennedy Presidential
Library and Museum*

8

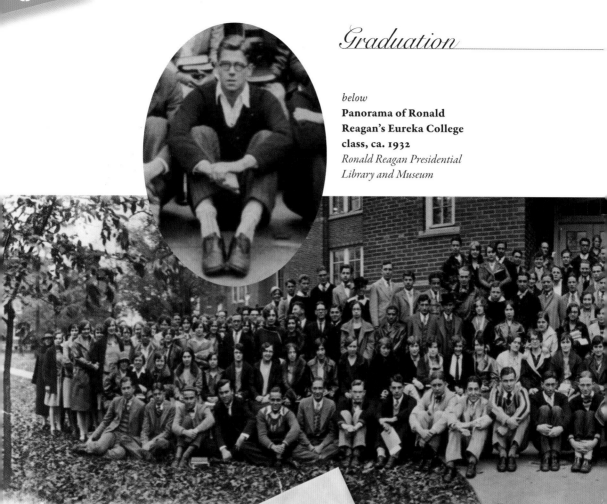

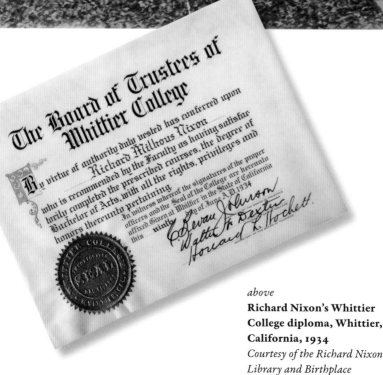

# Graduation

*below*
**Panorama of Ronald
Reagan's Eureka College
class, ca. 1932**
*Ronald Reagan Presidential
Library and Museum*

*above*
**Richard Nixon's Whittier
College diploma, Whittier,
California, 1934**
*Courtesy of the Richard Nixon
Library and Birthplace*

PRAESES ET SOCII
## UNIVERSITATIS YALENSIS
IN NOVO PORTU IN RE PUBLICA CONNECTICUTENSI OMNIBUS
AD QUOS HAE LITTERAE PERVENERINT SALUTEM IN DOMINO
SEMPITERNAM NOS PRAESES ET SOCII HUIUS UNIVERSITATIS
*George Herbert Walker Bush*
PRIMI HONORIS ACADEMICI CANDIDATUM AD GRADUM
TITULUMQUE ARTIUM LIBERALIUM BACCALAUREI ADMISIMUS
EIQUE CONCESSIMUS OMNIA IURA PRIVILEGIA INSIGNIA
AD HUNC HONOREM SPECTANTIA
IN CUIUS REI TESTIMONIUM HIS LITTERIS UNIVERSITATIS
SIGILLO IMPRESSIS NOS PRAESES ET SCRIBA ACADEMICUS
SUBSCRIPSIMUS a.d. XI KAL. IUL. MDCCCCXXXXVIII

SCRIBA

PRAESES

*left*
**George H.W. Bush's Yale diploma, written in Latin, 1948**
*George H.W. Bush Presidential Library and Museum*

*left*
**Graduation, United States Naval Academy, class of 1947, June 5, 1946**
*Courtesy of the Special Collections and Archives Division, Nimitz Library, U.S. Naval Academy*

*"Education is the most enduring legacy, vital to everything that we are and can become."*

George H.W. Bush

## Conclusion

As is the case for most of us, education and school-related activities were influential to the future Presidents and provided a foundation on which they built the rest of their lives. Whether in private school or public, whether growing up in a small town or a large city, each of our modern Presidents experienced a unique education that prepared him for leadership in the highest elected office in the land. Class photographs, written assignments, report cards, programs from extracurricular activities, and invitations to graduations help tell the story of America. These treasures of the National Archives Presidential Libraries demonstrate that future Presidents have shared in and will continue to share in the educational tradition of our nation. Access to the documentary heritage in the National Archives is the right of all Americans. These important records provide us with a greater understanding of our history and a better sense of our future. Just as each of our modern Presidents learned, graduated, and grew up into a larger world, we all have the opportunity to gain insight into our democracy through our own study of the historical material of our government and our leaders.